Open At The Top

Neal Vahle

Open At The Top
The Life of Ernest Holmes

Open View Press
Mill Valley, California

Open View Press
219 Beryl St.
Mill Valley, CA 94941
415-381-5875

Manufactured in the United States of America

Design, layout and print production management by David Johnson

First Printing, August, 1993, 5,000 copes

For Maria, Stephen, Thomas More & Peter

Acknowledgments

It would have been impossible to write this book without the active involvement of many key people in the Religious Science movement. I would like to acknowledge, in particular, Noel McInnis, who suggested the topic and put me in touch with officials at headquarters of the United Church of Religious Science in Los Angeles. Noel, who at the time was a minister at the National Science of Mind Center in Washington, D.C., provided continued advice and encouragement throughout the course of the project.

The support of the Interim Chief Operating Officer of the United Church of Religious Science, George St. Johns, and the communications staff, headed by Kathy Juline, was essential. By providing a stamp of approval to the thrust of my work, these staff officials—in addition to providing office space and clerical support—opened doors for me to some of Ernest Holmes' closest associates, the people whose testimony was essential for providing perspective, insight, and otherwise unattainable information.

I would like to give special thanks to Kathy Juline and her former associate on the publications staff, Larry Barber, for helping me develop interview questions, for suggesting people to interview, and for giving me feedback on the data I assembled. Glen Hayden, a longtime staff member took a personal interest in the project, suggested important topics to probe and served as a catalyst and sounding board. Albert Wickham, the church archivist provided access to the Holmes records, and pointed out valuable shortcuts in finding pertinent material.

➤

Marilyn Armor Leo and her mother, Mrs. Reginald Armor, gave valuable assistance by allowing me to have access to information contained in an unpublished biography of Holmes written in 1975 by Reginald Armor. Arthur Vergara, an editor with DeVorss & Company, and an expert on the New Thought and Religious Science movements, offered encouragement at a time when I was still undecided about proceeding with the project, and, in addition, gave freely of his wide knowledge and deep insight. G. Gordon Melton, of the University of California, Santa Barbara, a leading authority on the history of religions in America, suggested avenues of research and shared his knowledge of primary sources.

I was fortunate to have been able to draw from the wide knowledge of Elaine St. Johns, who knew Ernest Holmes personally through family connections since her youth, and who worked with Holmes himself in the last months of his life to develop material for what would have been his autobiography. St. Johns also assisted Fenwicke Holmes in the preparation of the 1970 biography of Holmes published by Dodd, Mead & Company.

Bill Lynn and the Reverend George Bendall, both young men in the 1950s, lived in the Holmes household during the last decade of Holmes' life and provided information available only to those with deep personal ties.

Several people involved in the Religious Science movement read the manuscript and offered valuable comments. These include the following ordained ministers: Carleton Whitehead, Craig Carter, Jack Addington, Fletcher Harding, William Hart, Marcia Sutton; and licensed practitioners Sarah Hargrave, Frieda Grinton and Vetura Papke.

Several editor/writer friends read the manuscript and gave freely of their advice. Former White House speech writer Milton Friedman, read the manuscript from the point of view of a critical outsider and identified several gaps that needed to be filled. Joy O'Rourke, my long-time associate at Heldref Publications, employed her editorial skills to suggest improvements in the presentation of the material. Finally, I want to thank Sue Cliff who proofread the manuscript and corrected errors.

While I have received generous support from friends and associates in attempting to present a mistake-free manuscript, I am aware that errors may still be present. For these I take full responsibility.

Contents

x

Foreword
by Carleton Whitehead D. D.

Open At The Top is thoroughly enjoyable reading. Dr. Neal Vahle had done an excellent job with a challenging subject. Mingling the results of exhaustive research and interviews with many of Dr. Ernest Holmes' close friends, Vahle has produced a story that is both factual and warmly personal.

The Ernest Holmes philosophy of Religious Science is clearly, accurately and succinctly presented directly from Vahle's research, without opinion from him or anyone else. It is fresh and vintage Holmes. Case histories of Spiritual Mind Treatment, written by Dr. Holmes for *Science of Mind* magazine, are extremely interesting and highly informative. So also are Holmes' views on the subject.

For the period prior to 1925 in Holmes' life there are few records available. Vahle had little choice but to rely on the biography of Holmes written by his brother Fenwicke entitled *Ernest Holmes: His Life and Times* (Dodd, Mead & Company, 1970). For the last thirty five years, however, of Ernest's life (he died in 1960), ample data is available from minutes of board meetings, church reports, articles, recordings, transcripts and eye-witness accounts. Vahle took full advantage of these. He really did his homework.

From the pages of *Open At The Top* a three dimensional colorful portrait of Ernest emerges — a warm, friendly, loving and lovable human being, a man with rare spiritual insight and a genius for coherently verbalizing his inner perceptions. These perceptions, enhanced by his communion with the spiritual giants of the past, lifted and enriched the lives of countless thousands who heard him speak and read his writings. Increasing numbers of people are likewise benefited as they continue to discover Dr. Holmes' timeless teaching.

➤

I particularly like this biography because the author was not personally acquainted with Dr. Holmes. Vahle is a trained historian with a Ph.D. in American History from Georgetown University. He thus has an unbiased approach. Previous accounts, written by persons very close to Ernest Holmes—his brother and a surrogate son—were quite naturally somewhat colored and incomplete. In these works a major chapter in Ernest's life was omitted—the episode that divided Religious Science into two separate organizations. In Vahle's work this episode, known as the "Split" in the Religious Science movement, is, in my opinion, appropriately treated.

Some who reviewed this manuscript objected on the grounds that it would put Dr. Holmes in an unfavorable light. I strongly disagree with this point of view. I was a personal friend of Holmes during the last ten years of his life, and he said many times, "When I'm gone, if they try to make me a saint, I'll come back and haunt them." A spiritual genius? Dr. Holmes certainly was one. He was not, however, one to hide a mistake or his own humanness.

On the evening of that fateful Friday, January 7, 1954, when the "Split" took place, Ernest expressed to me his feeling that the whole business was a tragic mistake. He would concur that this extremely important segment of his career belongs in his biography. Furthermore, at this critical phase in the history of the Religious Science movement, this momentous event needs to be known and understood.

I believe that Vahle's biography of Ernest Holmes is an exceedingly valuable addition to the Religious Science literature. It is *must* reading for everyone in this field. Neal Vahle is to be thanked and congratulated, not only for his excellent work in writing this biography, but also for his courage and persistence in publishing it in the face of strong resistance.

Carleton Whitehead is an ordained Religious Science minister who for the past forty years has been affiliated with Religious Science International. He also has served as President of that organization.

Preface
By Noel McInnis R. Sc. F.

Open At The Top is the only book of its kind. It features an overview of the Science of Mind philosophy, the life of its creator, Ernest Holmes, and the growth of the Religious Science movement from its inception to the time of Holmes' death.

Dr. Neal Vahle gives us an excellent representation of the Science of Mind philosophy, as what it is—a unique formulation of the universal principles of truth, distilled from the highest common denominators of the world's great religions, philosophies and mystical traditions, and focused on the task of establishing self-dominion (the reign of our Higher Self over our affairs).

The author also provides a glimpse (to use one of Holmes' own favorite verbal Trinities) of the "color, warmth and tone" of Science of Mind's creator, along with the highlights of his personal, intellectual and professional development.

Most admirably of all, Vahle has masterfully encountered the most difficult task of a Holmes biographer—to account for the bifurcation of Religious Science, with Holmes' unwitting yet palpable complicity, into two denominations. The "Split" took a highly unusual form for such occasions, since doctrine was never argued. I am certain that no one reporter's account of this event, Vahle's included, will fully accord the memories and feelings of all who were involved or subsequently informed. Yet this account bears the tone of an impartial witness. What more could we ask?

The author's straightforward and unbiased account performs a great service for our movement, for until now there has been no written account whatever for the Religious Science community of its most dramatic moment. No wonder that so many in each of our denominations remain ignorant of the other church's existence. This book ends our ignoring of this critical event.

➤

Vahle's work is as complete as the general audience of Religious Scientists and curious others would desire. Yet, anyone deeply engaged in the philosophy and community of Religious Science will probably find one or more statements that require qualification. This reflects no fault on the biographer, nor of anyone quoted. It merely acknowledges the rich diversity of our viewpoints.

Noel McInnis is an ordained minister with the United Church of Religious Science. He was co-founder and former co-minister with his wife, Rita, of the National Science of Mind Center in Washington, DC. Currently he is staff minister for education outreach at the Golden Gate Church of Religious Science in Marin County, CA.

CHAPTER I

It Was Not a Planned Thing

Nothing in Ernest Holmes' early life suggested that he would create a new spiritual philosophy, found a church which thousands would attend, inspire the "positive thinking" of Norman Vincent Peale which would spread through the churches of America. As a young man he gave little indication that he would influence the lives of several Hollywood personalities including Cecil B. DeMille, Peggy Lee, Cary Grant, and Robert Stack, and develop a technique of mental healing that would be a fore-runner of the mind-body modalities emerging in today's holistic medicine.

Born in 1887 he was raised in a rural New England family where religion played an important role. Yet as a youth, other than attending church and reading the Bible, he showed no strong affinity for organized religion. He did not excel in school. While he was an intelligent young man and showed an early interest in reading and learning, he found school itself dull and uninteresting, and left before finishing high school.

As a young adult he did not seek, as his older brother Fenwicke had sought, a career in the ministry. Moving from Maine to Boston at age eighteen he decided upon a career as a platform speaker and entertainer, and trained himself for it.

His discovery of Ralph Waldo Emerson, whose philosophical ideas were to become a major source of inspiration, came through a chance visit to the home of a family member where he stumbled upon a book of Emerson's essays. In Boston libraries he discovered the New Thought literature of Quimby, Dresser and Larsen, but gave no indication that he would do anything more with it than satisfy his own curiosity.[1]

In Boston he was introduced to the mental healing practices of Christian Science, when he was invited by a friend to attend Christian Science services. While he involved himself in the activities of the Mother Church in Boston, and attended lectures given by Mary Baker Eddy, he took no formal training to become a practitioner of Christian Science. Yet through reading, discussion and experimentation he developed a mental healing technique, similar in some respects to the healing practices of Christian Science. He called this technique Spiritual Mind Treatment. He practiced the technique with family and friends strictly as an avocation.

Holmes left Boston for California in 1912 at age twenty five. At that time he gave no indication that he would seek a career outside the entertainment field. He did not pursue Christian Science after arriving in California. He lived with his brother, Fenwicke, who was a Congregational minister in Venice (on the ocean 15 miles west of Los Angeles) and worked in the local community, first as a playground director and then as a city purchasing agent. Holmes spent his free time helping his brother with social activities in the church, reading further into New Thought literature, and giving mental healing to friends. His approach to metaphysical work was as an avocation rather than a profession.[2]

In Los Angeles he came across the works of the leading New Thought writer, Thomas Troward. Troward's work "eclipsed anything I ever read," he said, giving him further insight into the techniques of mental healing and the theory that lay behind it.

It was through fortuitous circumstance that Holmes moved toward a career in metaphysical teaching and healing. A co-worker at the purchasing office became interested in the metaphysical books he was reading and invited him to speak to a group of friends about what he had learned. He gave a series of lectures, speaking on the works of Troward. After the talks he gave Spiritual Mind Treatment for those who requested it.

An invitation to speak at the Metaphysical Library in Los Angeles came, not through self promotion, but on the recommendations of those who had heard him speak and who received mental healing from him. He left the work-a-day world for full time employment as a metaphysical teacher and healer after receiving increasing requests to speak and give Spiritual Mind Treatment. This made it possible to make a living at what he had heretofore considered a pastime.

When he began his metaphysical work he had yet to put together a coherent system of philosophical thought. Nevertheless, through reading, lecturing and healing practice, he was slowly but surely developing ideas that would form the basis of a spiritual philosophy which he was to call, "The Science of Mind." In 1916, with Fenwicke, he founded a metaphysical magazine called *Uplift.* He now had the opportunity to write, edit and immerse himself even more deeply in New Thought ideas and literature.

By 1917 he was speaking regularly on Sundays before growing crowds in Los Angeles theaters, and during the week teaching classes on metaphysics and working as a spiritual mind practitioner. It was during this period that he qualified himself for ordination as a minister of Divine Science, one of the New Thought churches. Recognizing that if he was to continue to be successful it was necessary to have writing to support his work, he began preparing manuscripts for two books. *Creative Mind* and *Creative Mind and Success* which were published in 1918.

He was making headway in permanently establishing himself when in 1918 he decided, at the suggestion of Fenwicke, to close down his work in Los Angeles, move back to the East Coast and lecture in New York and Philadelphia. Fenwicke, who had left the

Congregational ministry and joined Ernest in metaphysical practice, had traveled to the East coast to attend a conference of New Thought leaders and returned convinced that New York City was ripe for their metaphysical teaching.

Ernest's work on the East Coast was part of an eight year collaboration with Fenwicke. The brothers spent two years lecturing and giving Spiritual Mind Treatment. Apparently the work did not go as well as anticipated since they returned to Los Angeles in 1920. The next three years were spent attempting to re-establish the following that had been left behind two years before. They were unsuccessful, and, in 1923, the two men again left California for New England and New York. Fenwicke had more speaking engagements than Ernest, who spent much of his time preparing the book which was to become his first text in the philosophy of Religious Science. Entitled *Science of Mind*, the new book gave a fuller explanation of his philosophical ideas than his other writings.

In 1925 the Holmes brothers separated their work. Ernest returned to Los Angeles to strike out on his own while Fenwicke remained in the East. Ernest started over from scratch. When he began speaking in Los Angeles theaters he had no idea that a religious movement would soon flourish around him. He worked in the same way he had before leaving Los Angeles in 1918.

He taught classes on Science of Mind during the week, did Spiritual Mind Treatment for a growing clientele, and spoke on Sundays. In 1927 he began a new monthly magazine, which was first called Religious Science and then, two years later, *Science of Mind*. Like *Uplift* it provided literary support for his teaching. In that same year, 1927, he founded in Los Angeles the Institute for Religious Science and School of Philosophy and began training others to work as spiritual mind practitioners.

Within a short period of time his work was so popular that others sought to join him. Soon the Institute was training, not only Spiritual mind practitioners, but leaders who could replicate elsewhere the work Holmes was doing lecturing on Sundays and teaching during the week. Holmes actively helped these new leaders establish extensions of the Institute, first in localities in and around Los Angeles, and throughout the rest of the country. These groups were first called chapters of the Institute of Religious Science and Philosophy. In the 1940s they were renamed Churches of Religious Science.

The Religious Science movement, particularly during its first two decades, moved forward easily and spontaneously. As Holmes once said, "It was not a planned thing."

Holmes himself never stopped learning. He was constantly reading, exchanging ideas and searching. "Anything that comes along that is better than I have got," he once said, "I want to know about it." As a result his philosophy of Science of Mind was "open at the top", as he put it, for new insights, and for fresh and invigorating ways to present spiritual information.

Holmes married for the first and only time in 1927 at age forty. His wife, Hazel Foster Holmes, a wealthy well-connected Los Angeles socialite, became a practitioner of the work and provided invaluable support as a confidante and advisor. Her connections with established, important people in the business and entertainment community lent legitimacy to the work and contributed significantly to his success.

The Religious Science movement snowballed in the 1940s and 1950s and by the time Holmes died in 1960 there were 85 churches spread nation-wide as well as hundreds of licensed spiritual mind practitioners. Holmes never satisfactorily resolved the problems of organizing and administering a growing movement. At the time of his death there were two organizations, the United Church of Religious Science and Religious Science International, each claiming leadership of the movement.

Though lacking in organizational know-how, Holmes succeeded, throughout his long career, in doing the things he did best—preach on Sundays, teach his philosophy of Science of Mind, and practice Spiritual Mind Treatment.

CHAPTER II

As a Man Thinketh in His Heart So is He

Science of Mind

Holmes's teaching is based on a belief that there is a universal law of cause and effect operating in the life of humankind that is primarily mental and spiritual. Human beings have "conscious access to this law," he believed, through the correct use of thought, and thus can use this law for creative purposes. He was not overstating his belief in the power of thought when he said, "As a man thinketh in his heart, so is he."[1]

Holmes called his philosophy "Science of Mind."[.] In essence Science of Mind is a combination of philosophical ideas and spiritual practices. Spiritual Mind Treatment, the principal technique he developed, constituted, in his view, "a breakthrough in understanding and applying the ancient art and science of relating to the Infinite." Holmes summarized his philosophy of Science of Mind when he said, "The structure of our whole philosophy is based on two things: the Universe as law and order, and the universe as Divine Presence, the one with which or with whom we may commune, the other that we may use."

Holmes considered his philosophy to be a science because, "it can be taught, it can be learned, and it can be consciously applied with a certainty of definite and repeatable results." Holmes saw Science of Mind as "an intensely practical thing because it teaches us how to use the mind for definite purposes, such as helping those who are sick, impoverished or unhappy." He believed that everyone could benefit from becoming a practitioner of the art and a conscious user of its power.

When asked upon what authority his teaching was based, Holmes referred to Jesus, who, when asked the same question, said that the authority of his words were in his works. "There is no authority for Science of Mind," said Holmes, "other than what it accomplishes." The serious student of Science of Mind will discover "that it teaches a principle that can be demonstrated, that its authority is not in its words, but in what it can accomplish."

Holmes was once asked by a professor at the University of Southern California for a twenty-five word definition of Religious Science. The definition Holmes gave is as follows: "Religious Science is the correlation of laws of science, opinions of philosophy and revelations of religion applied to human needs and the aspirations of man."

The Nature of God and the Human Condition

Holmes's ideas on the nature of God were an essential part of his teaching. Holmes believed that in the universe there was "a Presence pervading all, an Intelligence running through all, and a Power sustaining all." Holmes identified God as "Universal Mind, Spirit, Intelligence, that is the origin of everything. . . . This Universal life and Energy finds an outlet in and through everything that lives."

Holmes did not believe in the trinitarian God of Christian teaching, which asserted the existence of three persons in one God—Father, Son and Holy Spirit. "God", said Holmes, "is not a person. God is a Presence." God was not a father figure who rewarded virtue and punished vice. "The Divine Parent," he said, "is not some far distant person, but a Universal Presence and Principle, already in our own soul, already operating through our own consciousness."

Too many people think of God "with the face and form of a man," he observed, "and picture Heaven as a place where he sits on a throne and you and I look at him and sing hymns." That idea of God repelled Holmes. "I look upon God," he said," as Intelligence of Mind everywhere present throughout the Universe and beyond the Universe." When we use the word "God," he said, "let us have it mean that Overshadowing Presence. . . . a Divine Intelligence that knows all things and can do all things."

Holmes did not view God as being outside, or over-and-above humankind. "There is a great difference," he noted, "in thinking of the Spirit as an inner rather than an over-lord. . . . If we think of the Spirit as an over-lord there is always an attempt to get up to it." It was most important to remember, he said, "that there is no God supervising a human kingdom." He once said, "I thank the God that *is* that the God that most people believe in *isn't*.

While Holmes made it clear that, while he did not believe God was a person to be worshipped, adored or obeyed, he acknowledged that "the great mystics of all ages have announced the personality of the Spirit. . . . They have all sensed the Divine as personal to them and have consciously communicated with it." This was not, he argued, "an anthropomorphic personalism," but a "Universal Consciousness, personal at the point of our contact with it." He granted, however, that the universe "did personify itself through man." Therefore, it was appropriate to think of God, "not only as Principle, forever pushing forward into expression, but as Infinite Person."

Holmes saw mankind as "unique representations of God. . . . Every man is a point of consciousness in God." The important thing, "the essence of faith," as he saw it, is that "there is a Presence and a Power to which we may turn, which always meets our needs if we believe." Holmes asserted that there was a "Divine nature in every man," something within us which "partakes of the nature of the Divine Being." Holmes believed that in spirit, "man is one with God". We must come to acknowledge, he said, "that God is all there is, and God is all that I am."

Throughout his lectures and writing, Holmes made the point, over and over again, that we, as human beings, "can find God only within ourselves." He acknowledged that this might seem "almost blasphemous, as though one were setting oneself up as God." Such was not the case, he argued. "One is merely setting oneself up as a center in the consciousness of God, forever one with God, an Incarnation of the Universal."

Holmes constantly preached that people should accept the fact that "the road to God is through the self. . . . The Supreme Being is at the center of each one of us. To it we may come for guidance, and from it we may draw inspiration and the power to live." Holmes believed it was totally wrong to conceive of God as a "Heavenly Dictator", something apart from that "which lives and moves and has its being where we are." If we viewed God as a Divine Despot we would become "disconnected from the Infinite Presence." The consequence of feeling subservient to God "would be a terrible fear that we should never be able to make contact with Him."

Holmes believed that the best way to commune with God was through prayers of recognition and affirmation. If we knew God as an "Indwelling Presence", then prayer would be naturally addressed "to the Presence in us." Prayer, he wrote, "is an act of the mind in the recognition of the Divine Presence, as a Universal Life Energy, Power, Intelligence and substance." He did not view prayer as supplication, or asking God for favors or help. "Prayer is not a petition to an unknown God to change the laws of his being because of the whimsical fancy of an individual." He lamented the fact that "most of our prayers are petition. . . . We pray that God will make the crops good, that he will cause rain to fall, that he will save the soul of some sinner."

The proper approach to prayer, Holmes believed, was to make it an effort "to so unify with the nature of Reality that nature shall automatically release its benevolence." Holmes argued that this approach was in alignment with the way Jesus taught his disciples to pray because it contained within it the key elements of recognition, identification and unification.

Holmes rejected the notion of an angry or punishing God. "There is no God anywhere," he said, "who wishes anyone harm. ... We should not listen to people who tell us we are depraved, that we are sinners, that we are sick, or that we are condemned." He was particularly critical of religious teaching that focused on the need for man to suffer to gain salvation. He believed it was "false and morbid" to view God as a being "who does not want us to have anything, who makes us suffer and suffer and suffer, and who places us here to learn through hardship."

Holmes did not deny the fact of human suffering. "We do suffer," he said, "but only through ignorance. If we can turn from ignorance to enlightenment, suffering will cease. That can happen in a moment." More so than maliciousness or spite, Holmes believed that ignorance or faulty thinking were the source of human difficulty. He once said, "I believe that most of our troubles arise, not so much from maliciousness, as from ignorance."

Holmes lamented the fact that society as a whole has been "afraid of God. . . . afraid of being spiritual." He suggested that we have mistrusted religious sentiment because we have misinterpreted it. "Religion is really a life, not a creed," he said, "an atmosphere, not an object. We are afraid of Spirit because we have divorced life from living. . . . Only when the thought about God becomes normal as the thought about sun and rain will the Universal Spirit be really with us." Holmes named a few exceptional human beings—Jesus, Emerson, Buddha and Walt Whitman— whose lives showed no fear of God. These humans understood that "there was nothing in the Universe to be afraid of." They knew that "the worst thing we shall ever be attacked by forever is our own imagination."

Holmes firmly believed in the immortality of the human soul. "Death loses its sting, and the grave its victory," he said, "when we realize the eternity of our own being." Holmes was completely convinced that "there is a spiritual body within us now, actually sustaining the physical, and that all death means is the severance of the one from the other." Every man, he said, "is an incarnation of

Life, of God, and it is inconceivable that Life, which is God, could ever cease to be."

Holmes did not believe in reincarnation. He felt that after death the soul moved to another form of life, but it did not return to life on earth. "I am certain, he stated, "that people pass from this world to the next completely as they were, except that they are no longer using this physical body." They did not return, however, in another body, to experience human life again. "I do not believe that people return to this world again by way of reincarnation. I believe that there are other worlds or planes, whatsoever you choose to call them, which are just as tangible and real as this one."

Holmes did not take a fixed position on the subject and saw no harm if people believed that they would reincarnate. He told Frieda Grinton, an Institute practitioner, that if belief in reincarnation helped anyone "become the person that they were meant to be spiritually," then, by all means, believe in it. For himself, however, he could not accept it. "To believe in Reincarnation is to believe that God is limited," he said, "and I believe that God is limitless." In a pixie manner that was so characteristic of him, he told Grinton, "I'll tell you this much, they've gotten the last pair of diapers on me they are ever going to get."

Holmes believed that after death one would meet those with whom they had been associated in this life, and that their work would continue. "We may confidently expect to meet friends on the other side and to know and be known when we shall meet." The meeting place he called "heaven" and indicated that he believed it would be a very active place. "We should not look forward to a heaven where there shall be nothing to do, but a place where our work will be done in greater harmony with the Divine Law because of a better understanding of it."

Holmes believed it was impossible for a soul to go to hell after death. "Humanity has been hypnotized," he said, "into a belief in hell." He did not believe that God punished people for sin after death. He viewed it as tragic that humankind "has suffered untold agony from something that has no existence outside its own imagination." If there was a hell, Holmes said, it existed here on earth, in the minds of those people who "insist in their ignorance in living contrary to the nature of reality." For those persons who make "negative use of the creative power of thought" life could indeed be a hell of their own making.

The best hope for those people who suffer because of their strong belief in the existence of hell, was an attitude of forgiveness, not only of others, but of themselves. "I have never known anyone," he stated, "no matter how fantastic his idea of future punishment may have been, who has not been healed in such degree as he learns to forgive himself and others. As he does this, and learns to become inwardly kind, his thought about hell, the devil and future punishment changes."

Holmes has been criticized for leaving love out of his teaching. While love was not a topic he focused on as much as "The Law" there are occasional references to love throughout his writing. "In an intelligent study of the teachings of the Science of Mind," he said, "we come to understand that all is love and yet all is law. Love rules through Law. Love is the Divine Givingness. Law is the way. Love is spontaneous. Law is impersonal...Love points the way, and Law makes the way possible." At another place in his writings he commented that "We live in a Universe of Love as well as a Universe of Law. One is the complement of the other." Holmes himself was a warm, affectionate and loving human being. It is surprising that he did not address the importance of love in more depth in his teachings.

Holmes seems to have been of two minds about the question of the existence of evil in the Universe. He made several statements that indicate he believed evil had no existence and was merely a figment of humankind's imagination. "The illumined have all known," he said, "that there is no final evil in the Universe.... What we should realize, is that any evil, any lack, any limitation, any negative whatsoever, which has appeared in our experience, will disappear just as soon, and completely, as we no longer contemplate it, believe in it, think about it, or give it any power." He went on further to state that it would be impossible for us to gain a sense of union with God if we believed in "the devil, hell and final evil."

From the following statements a reader might conclude that Holmes did indeed believe in the reality of evil. "Evil is an experience of the human being," he said, "if by evil we mean sickness, want, lack, impoverishment, unhappiness or physical deterioration. . . . We do not deny that people experience what we call evil, for such a denial would be absurd. . . . The origin of evil is in the human mind...The belief must be erased from the mind. We must come to know that there is no ultimate evil."

The Law of Mind and Spiritual Mind Treatment

One of the basic propositions in Holmes teaching was that "we live in a mental or spiritual universe," and that universe is governed by a law of cause and effect. He referred to the law of cause and effect as "The Law of Mind." This law "is set in motion consciously," said Holmes, "through the power of human thought." It operates automatically. "Its reaction is mechanical and mathematical."

Because of the existence of the Law of Mind, Holmes placed great stress on the importance of the power of thought. He believed that whatever happened in our lives, for good or ill, was the direct result of our thinking. There was a direct relationship "between thought and environment." Humankind's primary difficulty lay in the fact that most people's thoughts were largely negative. The Law of Mind reflected those thoughts back into man's experience by producing physical and emotional illness.

Holmes listed worry, fear, doubt, anger, jealousy, morbidity and guilt as examples of negative thoughts and emotions that are "back of most of our troubles." Each is "mental in nature." Operating through the Law of Mind they are "the hidden cause of a large part of all physical suffering to which the flesh is heir." Since the Law of Mind dictated "all mind activity inevitably tends to create its physical correspondent," it was not surprising that physical and emotional difficulties arose out of what Holmes characterized as "unhealthy or morbid mental states."

Holmes recognized that it was difficult to control thoughts. "It is not easy in the midst of pain," he said, "to think peace, in the midst of poverty to think abundance, in the midst of unhappiness to think joy."

Nevertheless, the control of thought was essential. The Law of Mind could be used for positive purposes. Man, should "look to the mind for the answer to all of our problems", because, man, by thinking, "can bring into his experience whatsoever he desires, if he thinks correctly." To learn to think was "to learn how to live." The point could not be overemphasized. "The Science of Mind was the science of right thinking."

The Law of Mind, "when rightly used," said Holmes, irresistibly draws us toward the object of our desires. "One of the most comforting ideas ever entertained," said Holmes, was that thought could be used creatively to produce good in our lives.

Spiritual Mind Treatment was the technique developed by Holmes to use the Law of Mind positively and creatively to change our lives for the better. This practice sets in motion "The Law of Mind" for the express purpose of changing situations and improving conditions, and, according to Holmes for bringing into "actual manifestation the health and happiness which are mankind's normal and divine heritage." Holmes called Treatment "the science of inducing within the mind concepts, acceptances and realizations of peace, poise, power, and plenty—health, happiness, and success—or whatever the particular need may be." When we treat, Holmes said, "we do something to our minds to convert them to a new belief, from a belief in evil to a belief in good, from a belief in lack to a belief in abundance, from a belief in fear to faith."

While it was most commonly used for physical or emotional healing, Treatment could be used for a multiplicity of purposes, and in a wide variety of life circumstances. Someone once asked Holmes, "But does it apply if I want to buy an automobile, a house or a dress?" His answer was "yes, why not?" There is no big and little. There is nothing more important than something else. It is right that we should be happy." There is no difference, he said, "between treating somebody for physical healing and treating somebody for the manifestation of money. Both acts are purely mental."

Emphasizing the point, he stated, "The thing you and I desire to fulfill life is important.... Anything that gives you pleasure today and harms no one is important.... Therefore I say that anything that you want, as long as it is in line with that which is constructive, cannot have any harm in it, and we have a perfect right to try to get it."

While there are no hard and fast rules and no ritual to repeat, there are a series of distinct and separate steps which needed to be taken. These included:

Recognition

This involves recognizing that there is a power in the Universe greater than we are. It involves knowing that there is a "Divine Mind" or "Infinite Intelligence" which operates, "in and through and back of the world in which we live." The person treating should bring themselves to an inner place where, according to Holmes, "there is no misfortune, no calamity, no accident, no trouble, no confusion, where there is nothing but plenty, peace, power, Life and Truth."

Identification

This involves recognizing that "we are a part of God.... We identify ourselves with God by a conscious, intelligent sensing and feeling of the Divine Presence within." In this step there is a deep knowing that we are one with God, that there is no separation between us and God.

Declaration

Here we declare our intention, or make a statement of desire or want. Holmes called it, "voicing, in thought, what we desire in some aspect of our life." Holmes advised that these declarations should be "definite, clear and specific". It was through our declaration "that we establish our desire as an entity in the spiritual realm of causation." There must be a deep inner knowing that the statements made are true, and thoughts must be in accord with words used. Holmes emphasized the importance of the declaration when he said, "Whatever power there may be in Spiritual Mind Treatment, whatever effectiveness it may have, results from the emphatic nature of the declaration."

Acceptance

When there is true acceptance there is a deep inward sense of peace and trust, and a complete conviction that there is a Law of Mind that works for us. There is an accompanying belief that the good we desire is "being manifest now." Holmes said that "we can specifically declare the good we desire time and time again, but until we are able to accept that good as being ours now, not at some future time, it will forever be a nebulous dream." Holmes also advised that in our acceptance there must be an expression of thanks, a feeling of gratitude for that which has taken place.

For the Treatment to have "strength and vitality" it was important that recognition, identification, declaration and acceptance flow freely and spontaneously into the mind rather than from a prepared statement or out of rote memory. It was important that there was "an easy, consistent flow of thinking, that is convinced of the truth of what is being thought." The words themselves weren't critical. "It was what one believes when one says it that counts." The person must believe that the treatment will work. A successful treatment, according to Holmes, embodied "an unqualified faith that the Law works for us as we work with it."

Holmes said that the "primary first step in spiritual mind healing is an awareness of God." The person who got the best results, he observed, was "the one who has the most complete conviction of the Divine Presence, and the deepest consciousness of spiritual harmony." If you watch yourself, he noted, "you will see that the effectiveness of your treatment will depend on how much of an embodiment there was of love, or compassion of life, and of what I choose to call the abandonment of the mind and soul to the Spirit." A realization of the Presence of God, Holmes concluded, "is the most powerful healing agency known to the mind of man."

Strong conviction was also essential. When one gives Treatment, Holmes said, one "is not sitting around hoping that something may happen." The person is "definitely, constructively, actively stating, sensing and knowing some specific good."

Holmes also pointed out that there was no mental coercion in Treatment. "You do not will things to happen". Rather it is a "mental awareness, a spiritual awareness of the mind. The mind is endeavoring to see the result as already accomplished, to believe that it is already done."

Holmes was emphatic on the importance of getting results. "Our work rests entirely upon demonstration," he said, "and the kind of demonstration we believe in is the kind that can be checked by a physician. . . . If we are treating for the removal of a cancer, we have not made a demonstration until the cancer is gone." Treatment should be repeated until the result is obtained. "If the thought is not manifesting in our experience, we should work until it does."

Holmes saw a clear distinction between treatment and pastoral counseling. His friend Bill Lynn reports that Holmes believed there was no need for ministers to go through orthodox counseling procedures. He himself was not interested in counseling. If you had a problem, Lynn recalls, Holmes would treat for it, and he did not need to know the details about the difficulty.

Practicing Spiritual Mind Treatment For Others

Holmes encouraged all with whom he came into contact to learn to practice Spiritual Mind Treatment. Membership in the Church of Religious Science was not a prerequisite. Anyone, he said, "who attempts to heal himself or another through a recognition of the creative power of mind and the ever availability of Good is a mental or spiritual practitioner." Anyone can heal, he said, "who believes he can, and who will take the time to set that belief in motion through the Law."

While it was possible to practice Treatment for oneself, it worked best when one person treated for another. Holmes encouraged people to become professional practitioners of Spiritual Mind Treatment, and to make a livelihood at it, much the same as a medical doctor or psychiatrist. As Dean of the Institute of Religious Science and Philosophy he wanted to have many, many people learn how to treat. Holmes established a training program to enable people to qualify as professionals in the practice, and every year the Institute graduated and licensed several practitioners.

Holmes exhorted his students upon graduation, telling them, "Now go out and heal. Do the Thing. Be the Thing Itself." Professionals, he said, should dedicate their lives, time, energies and intelligence "to helping others through mental and spiritual means and methods." Much of his teaching was directed towards those who worked professionally, and his writing on the subject of treatment often focused on the practitioner's role in treating clients.

Holmes assured his practitioners that if treatment was done correctly the Law of Mind would be activated and negative thought would "pass out of the consciousness of the patient." It was the effective use of Spiritual Mind Treatment that Holmes referred to when he said, "There is a power in the universe greater than you are and you can use it."

Spiritual Mind Treatment was the central focus of Holmes's professional life. The Dean of the church's College of Ministers, Fletcher Harding stated that Treatment was the basis of the Religious Science movement under Holmes, and that his concept of Treatment was his major contribution to the metaphysical movement. Vetura Papke, who for several years served under Holmes as the head of the practitioner group at the Institute in Los Angeles, agreed. "At heart, "said Papke, "Holmes was a practitioner. Treatment was his teaching." Holmes himself emphasized the importance of Treatment when he told Religious Science minister, Craig Carter, "We are a teaching order and a healing order, rather than a preaching order."

The reports of several people who knew Holmes personally indicate that he himself was a very effective practitioner. He would treat for any personal problem and was confident that, if he did it correctly, there could be miraculous results. Vetura Papke reported that Holmes continually got good results and he had clients throughout his lifetime from the movie industry and business community. In several articles in *Science of Mind* magazine, Holmes described the work he did with specific clients. In the following stories, published in the magazine, Holmes told in his own words how he treated.

She Couldn't Get Pupils

She taught piano, and, I think was a very good teacher. But she was in a good business to starve to death. At any rate, she couldn't seem to get pupils.

This particular person had been a student of the New Thought for many years and naturally part of her discouragement she attributed to the thought that it was impossible for her to make an adequate demonstration. She couldn't understand why she had not been able to manifest supply through the natural channel of her chosen profession.

Upon examining her thought, I discovered that all the statements she made in treatment were abstract. That is she was always saying, "God is all there is. God is the only Mind there is. God is the only Presence there is." But these statements were never brought into a clear and definite outline in her consciousness, that is, they had no real meaning to her. She labored under the misapprehension that abstract statements can produce definite results. No greater mistake could be made in our Science.

We must always connect the Principle with what we are doing and since our work is in the field of consciousness alone, we must make this connection definitely and consciously in our imagination. That is, if one is making a statement that "there is One Life and that Life is God," he should complete the statement by saying, "That Life is my life now." An artist does not take a lot of different paints and say, "These are the kind of materials which I use in the creation of pictures." He mixes these paints according to his desire and imagination and definitely draws a picture.

Using materials which existed before his need of them arose, he forms them into definite shape and does specific things with them.

One of the great troubles which we discover in so many persons' experience in this Science is that they fail to do this in giving mental treatments. The statement that God is all there is, is a statement of belief. It is a statement of the Principle we are convinced is true. That statement was true before we ever made it; it would remain true if we were never conscious of it. But if we want the Principle to do anything for us, we must have a definite concept.

I told this teacher of music that this was what she had failed to do. She had been going around making a lot of abstract statements, but never connecting them up with her own definite activity.

"But," she said, "I thought we were not supposed to outline." I explained the difference between outline and choice. We certainly do not have to outline the specific way in which a demonstration is to take place, else how can the power flow to us? In treatment we specialize the Principle for definite purposes. As a matter of fact, this is what constitutes scientific use of the Mind Principle. And we shall never receive any specific results unless we adhere to this practice.

I told her that since she was an individual she had a perfect right to her individual use of the Creative Principle. I told her that if her desire was to teach the piano, then she should know that the Creative Principle was unifying her with those whom she could peculiarly benefit. This she had never done. That was why she had failed to demonstrate.

Building upon the conviction she already possessed, I taught her to treat more after the following: "I have a service to render. My business is to teach the piano. Whoever needs my service, whomever I can peculiarly and personally benefit, all those whom I can particularly aid in this art, are irresistibly drawn to me now, today, this moment."

There is no state of futurity in Mind, therefore all statements should be an affirmation of the present. I taught her to live in the expectancy that wherever she went she would meet people who would desire her assistance, who would be glad to have it, and who would be able to justly compensate for her services. This was an entirely new line-up and one she had never thought of or used before. I taught her that her belief in the Infinite was right, her statements about God were correct, but that she had not completed her treatment, that in a certain sense she hadn't joined heaven and earth into one harmonious unity. I taught her to expect to meet people wherever she went who would require her services.

It was very interesting to have the privilege of observing the direct results which followed. After a few months she told me that it was the most remarkable thing she had ever experienced. She would go into a restaurant and sit down beside a stranger and in the course of conversation she would be asked what was her profession, or what did she do, and then she would tell him. On quite a number of occasions in just this way she secured pupils. She found pupils at parties, in the theater, on the street. All at once her friends seemed to remember what her profession was and began to send pupils to her. She soon became very busy in her chosen activity and I am sure that she had learned a lesson which we all must learn — that we specialize in a universal Principle for definite purposes; that just a statement about this Principle is not sufficient.

Of course I taught her that there is no magic in any formula, but nevertheless, certain mental methods of procedure, persisted in and believed, must produce definite results. Naturally, her thought was centered around the desire to express in her chosen field. She already had this atmosphere around her, but she had never connected the idea that the statement of Principle must be followed by definite direction. As soon as she began to see that Creative Principle was bringing her pupils, It began to do so. She had had the power, but had failed to use it.

He Was Too Fat

When I sat down beside him my first thought was, "What a very fat boy.'" He was about sixteen and was in a very critical condition. This boy happened to be a Catholic, but of course, it makes no difference to us what anyone's particular religious convictions may be. The average Catholic has a very childlike trust which is wonderful to build on. Theological differences play no part whatsoever in scientific spiritual mind healing. As a matter of fact, I was glad the boy was a devout Catholic, for at least he had some faith to lay hold of.

He had received a serious injury to his kidneys in an automobile accident and it was thought that he could not possibly live. The nurse told me that he was gradually filling up with water. We all know what the end result of the condition would be.

I had a long talk with him on my first visit and discovered that he had already been told that he could live but a short time. He was an interesting lad, with not too much education, but there never seemed to be anything morbid about him. I remember asking him on my first visit if he thought he was going to die. He said, "I suppose so."

"Well," I said, "are you afraid to die?"

He said, "Oh, no. I have lived a clean life and of course I believe in immortality."

We talked about that quite a bit and I was thoroughly convinced that he had no fear of making the transition. I told him I thought it was more in the nature of a resurrection, that I felt when people leave the world they immediately go into another objective environment and continue on much as they were in this, that I didn't think there was anything to be afraid of. He quite agreed with all this and felt everything would be well with him.

Well, that is where the case rested. But just before I got up to go he said, "But Mr. Holmes, why should I have to die at this time? Why couldn't I be well and live a normal, natural life?"

"But," I said, "haven't you been told that your time is very near at hand?"

"Yes," he said, "but somehow or other I don't believe it."

I pointed out to him that he had received a very severe injury to his kidneys and that there was no human hope for his recovery.

"Yes," he said, "Mr. Holmes, but I thought you believed in something different. You know, my aunt, who is a nurse and who is taking care of me, goes to your lecture and she has told me that she is confident I can be healed."

"And do you wish so greatly to get well?" I asked.

"Of course," he said. "Why shouldn't I? I have the same desires that any other boy would have. I would like to be well and happy and do all those things a person naturally should do in this world."

"And just what," I asked, "do you think would be the power that could heal you?"

His reply was most revealing. He said, "Something made my body, didn't it?"

"Yes," I answered.

"Well, that is God, isn't it?" he asked.

"Of course," I said. "God makes everything."

His next remark was excellent and really what I had been waiting for, hoping to get and somehow or other subconsciously I expected him to say just what he did say, which was this: "If God made my kidneys in the first place, why couldn't he remake them?"

Now, what would you do in a case like that? You couldn't very well say, "No." Therefore you would have to say, "Yes, of course God can make as many kidneys as He wishes to."

This all may seem like rather childlike prattle, but remember, this boy was at death's door and he wasn't afraid. He was dying and it didn't seem to matter so much to him, but somehow the age-old question popped up in his imagination: "What is it all about, anyway?"

I said to him. "Let us believe that God is going to heal you. Let's believe that the Spirit in you is going to eliminate everything from your physical body which doesn't belong to it."

Well, we set to work on this proposition, taking the line of thought that whatever there was in him that didn't belong would be eliminated and that every natural and normal channel for this elimination was in complete and full force. I worked on the thought that since the Spirit had created proper organs for elimination, these organs must be spiritual and of course the Spirit cannot fail properly to function. The physical manifestation of this Divine Idea may have been impaired, but its subjective image is never destroyed.

A very interesting thing followed. He didn't die, he got well. The process of his recovery was interesting, and to me enlightening. I had taken the thought that whatever was in him that didn't belong would be eliminated and that every organ necessary for this activity would function perfectly. Of course I never looked inside the boy. I made no physical examination, for that isn't our office. He was being attended by a fine and competent physician who very graciously cooperated with me in every respect. He was being attended by a trained nurse and had the loving care of a family devoted to his good. But it was interesting to me to observe what followed.

He began to perspire very freely and in a few days his kidneys began to operate. Many quarts of liquid were discharged through these two processes of elimination within the next few days. He was no longer a fat boy. As a matter of fact, he was quite thin and emaciated. This process went on for about two weeks, but there still seemed to be something there that didn't belong.

I continued my work for about a month and while there had been great signs of improvement for the first few weeks, the month that followed brought but little hope for his recovery. He had very severe pains in his body and something settled in the region of his thigh, something which wouldn't eliminate. I remember it was Thanksgiving morning when I was again called to his bedside. He was suffering very severe pain and he said, "Isn't there something you can do about it?"

I replied that we would try for him to be as calm as possible and I would devote all the time I could spend that day to treatment. I know I went home and made myself comfortable and again took up the thought that whatever there was in him that didn't belong, would be eliminated. It was the only thought that seemed to have any meaning to me. And thoughts without meaning have no power.

I worked with this thought, I suppose, for several hours. That night two openings appeared and a very large amount of pus was discharged. Whatever the pressure had been which caused his severe pain, was eliminated in this way. From then on his recovery was very rapid. In a few weeks he was up and shortly after that back in school.

This happened years ago and so far as I know he never had any recurrence of this trouble. A miracle, you say? Possibly. I don't know. Rather, I would say the miracle of Life itself. I hope whoever reads this article will realize that there is no peculiar thing which we have to teach, no personal doctrine, no individual truth. This thing really happened and I haven't the slightest doubt that you or anyone else could have accomplished the same results in a similar case if you would take the time to induce the same belief.

Perhaps you will say, "What do you mean by inducing a belief? My answer is, I mean exactly what I say; that if one works with himself consistently and persistently, using statements which convey the proper meaning to his own mind, something happens. My belief is that if not quickly, then gradually, an inner subjective embodiment of the idea stated takes form, and I believe that this inner subjective embodiment sets the creative Law in motion for the definite purpose specified.

This may not seem like much of an explanation, but I feel it is the true one. Do you wish to call this "faith"? I am content. Would you prefer the word "prayer"? I will not deny your conviction. But if you choose to think that repeated statements, finally believed in, lay hold of some invisible Law of Cause and Effect, which operates in human affairs, I am prepared to say, "Amen."

I Am Too Old To Succeed

His daughter had been healed of a lung infection, so already he had proof of the pudding which comes only with the eating. He came in one evening to inquire if the same Power that had brought about his daughter's healing, which had seemed to him so miraculous, could not do something for him in a financial way.

I explained to him that what had appeared to him as a miracle was a divinely natural thing and that Life Itself is a miracle. Walt Whitman said a blade of grass was miracle enough for him. Of course it is difficult for people who haven't tried to figure these things out, to understand the simplicity of it all, the direct approach which we should have to this great Principle of our being, this ever-present Something to which we have given the name God.

This man, however, was rather a religious type, and, I believe, had implicit faith and confidence in spiritual things. At any rate, his daughter had been healed of a very serious condition and it seems that he had been pondering this over in his mind for several months until at last the thought came to him, why couldn't this same Power do something for him in a business way?

He was sixty-five years of age and was driving a cart, delivering bakery products to the retail trade. I believe he was making about eighteen dollars a week. At one time he had owned his own store and had conducted a successful business, but like many others, conditions had changed and his business was lost. It had become necessary for him to do the best he could to support himself and his wife.

His first remark was: *"Any power which is wonderful enough to have healed my daughter surely can do anything."*

"Yes," I replied, *"the Power certainly can do anything. It is up to us, however, to realize that It is doing it."*

I tried to explain to him that this is a simple matter of the Law of Cause and Effect, which happens to be mental and spiritual rather than physical. I pointed out to him that we are surrounded by a Creative Principle which, because of Its very nature, is always receiving our thought impulses and doing something with them. Naturally, he came back with the remark that he had never expected to fail and how could his failure have been in his own mind.

I guess this is a question which we all ask somewhere along the road and it has always seemed to me a perfectly legitimate one. I never have believed in taking the attitude that something must be wrong with us because we are sick, poor or unhappy. Personally, I prefer the more impersonal attitude that ignorance is the only sin there is and the reward of ignorance is what we call punishment. I am a great believer that there is no sin but a mistake and no punishment but a consequence. It seems to me that this takes care of everything and leaves each one of us free to work out his own salvation with neither fear nor trembling, but with the will to understand things as they are, to accept them as they must be, and to try and remold our outlook on life to a more Divine pattern.

At any rate, I think I succeeded in explaining to this man that he should have no sense of condemnation because he had failed. Millions of others had failed before him. There was nothing vicious about this. It was merely a condition and I explained to him that there was a Silent Cause at work in the innermost resources of his own thought. I pointed out to him that there is a Divine Presence within everyone and around everyone which may be relied upon. I tried to show him that this Divine Presence is personal to each one of us, that he could talk to It as he drove his bread wagon, delivered his rolls and cakes.

Perhaps the most difficult thing to get him to see was that this Principle upon which he must learn to rely, is independent of any existing circumstance. It created every business that was ever conducted and could just as well present him with a new one. But first he must believe. I don't think his position was any different from that of any of us. We really live by faith, whether we are conscious of it or not. We may call this faith, philosophy, religion, or science, personal conduct or human behavior— what's in a name? One thing is certain—we must believe.

I don't think I have ever met a man who more readily came to believe than he did. He had an almost boyish enthusiasm in his new outlook on life. He was going out to win. Never once in the three months that followed did he falter; I never heard him make a negative remark about himself after our first evening's conversation. He came to me regularly. Nothing much seemed to happen for quite a while. I was working every day to know, and he was cooperating with me, that that which would be best suited to him, which would best protect him, which would give him the best outlet for whatever capacities he had, that thing would be shown to him, it would be presented to him in such a definite way he could not misunderstand or misinterpret. But no tangible result appeared, as I remember, for several months.

Now it so happened that on his route my friend delivered bakery goods to a small but successful store, owned by a man about his own age, in a neighborhood location in one of our beach cities here in Southern California. This man owned his own building and his entire stock. He had made a neat little fortune, but had never retired from business. One day my friend called to deliver some goods and the proprietor of this store asked him if he had ever had any experience in the grocery business.

Naturally this was just down his alley, so to speak, and he said "I certainly have. It has been my business all my life. I used to have a store of my until a few years ago, but you know. . .   "Well," said the proprietor of the store, "how would you like to come and work for me? I will pay you whatever you are making on the wagon. I think you will find it easier and probably more to your liking."

Of course he gladly accepted this position. Several months followed, when one day the owner of the store said to my friend, "I would like to turn this building, this business and the entire stock over to you and let you run it on your own. You may pay me for it out of the profits of the business. I know you will make a success of it and I know that I shall receive my full compensation in due time."

The man was radiant when he told me this story and I couldn't help but rejoice with him, thinking how wonderful are the secret ways and the *invisible processes of this Principle which we are privileged to use. The man became successful and the Law of Cause and Effect measured out to him, well filled and running over, everything which he had a mental equivalent. It could not do more; It would not do less.*

Voices Called To Her

She was a woman about sixty, cultured, traveled, and educated. Several years before I met her, her only brother, who had been a splendid business executive and a money maker, had been resurrected from this life into the next one. She was amply provided for financially and appeared to have good business judgment in handling her affairs. But with it all, she was one of the most pathetic figures I have ever seen.

Voices talked to her. It seemed as though invisible entities were tormenting her. If I had ever believed in spirit obsession—which I never have—I should have felt that she was really obsessed. It seems that some months before I met her, she had learned to use a ouiji board and was delighted with the messages which she received. They were beautiful, helpful, kindly, and, as a matter of fact, contained considerable philosophic discussion of no little merit.

Gradually, in her psychic development, she found that she could dispense with the ouiji board and communicate directly with these alleged invisible presences. Everything was happy as a lark. She was elated over her new discovery. But the day came when these voices, which up until then had been so kindly, and these presences, which had been so benign, became quite vicious. They began to persecute her, to tell her that because of sins she had committed, she must be punished until the sins were atone for.

She did her best to bear up under what seemed to her a just demand, but presently these influences, or whatever we may choose to call them, took a more vicious turn. It would be impossible for me to state just how she felt inwardly, but I am convinced that her experiences were real enough, so far as she was concerned. She used to tell me that she suffered actual physical pain as a result of the persecutions; she was not allowed to sleep at night.

Her torment had really reached an excruciating stage and it was my privilege to deliver her from whatever anyone may choose to call the condition she was in. At first I tried to explain to her that these voices were really her own subconscious self; that perhaps she had some deep-seated but unconscious sense of guilt, and that this was the way her mind was taking to condemn her. I don't think she had ever done anything very bad in her life, but so often we find well-meaning, honest and constructive people, who entertain this deep sense of guilt. I have often felt that it might arise from the race consciousness itself, the theological condemnation of the ages, a misuse of conscience, a misconception of the beautiful relationship which the soul should have to the universe.

I have found it impossible to get anywhere with this method of procedure. She used to say, "It isn't anything in me, Mr. Holmes. I am dealing with some very vicious entities and I shall lose my reason if this goes on. Either they must be destroyed or I shall be." Naturally, she feared insanity.

Finding it impossible objectively to explain to her what I believed to be the seat of her trouble, I began a process of silent treatment which I felt sure would deliver her from her torment. I was thoroughly convinced then, and still am, that she was talking to herself.

I took the line of thought that since there is but One Spirit, One Mind, and One Divine Purpose in life, which is complete and happy, and since each of us is an individual center of this God-Consciousness, that there wasn't anything in reality that could torment her. I reasoned that there was no power, no person, or presence in the flesh or out of it, which could obsess, possess, or suggest anything to her, good, bad, or indifferent. I took the thought that the One Mind controlled her and that the whole theory of spirit obsession or of the obsession of mental suggestion, was entirely foreign to the Truth, could not operate through her, had no power over her, no reality and no appearance of reality.

The thing didn't happen in a minute. Her trouble was very deep-seated and it took some time for her to find a complete emancipation, but gradually the influences waned, the voices grew less distinct. I kept right on with what I believed to be the correct mental explanation, that there is but One Mind. I kept on knowing within myself that she must come to realize that she had merely been talking to herself. I worked to know that *she would consciously see this and understand it. One day when I called upon her—for her condition had been such that she couldn't come to the office—she met me at the door with a joyous expression on her face. She said, "You know, I have had the most wonderful experience. I know that I am going to be healed." Last night, she said, "the voices told me that there were not people at all; that I have been laboring under an hallucination and that you were entirely right, It has been my own subjective self that has been talking to me."*

Of course I knew that she was healed. For the true explanation had consciously come to her thought, that which I had been working on for weeks was now revealed to her mind. The healing was complete and permanent. Possibly some of you who read this article will believe that she actually was obsessed by discarnate entitites. Personally, I do not like to take this viewpoint. But I know this: whatever it was which obsessed her, acted as though they were entities. I am inclined to take the position that it was a case of multiple personality, a split in the subconscious where it sometimes appears as though fragments of the mind were sheared off from the main body of thought and therefore react with apparent individual intelligence. In her case the integration was complete.

I Will Set Him On High Because He Hath Known My Name"

In this case it wasn't a "him" at all. It happened to be a young woman who was trying to break into the motion picture profession. She was young, inexperienced, and apparently knew of no objective way of crashing the gates. It would be improper to reveal her name, since she is now known around the world. Of course, she must have had native ability else it never could have happened. We certainly have no system which transforms a cabbage into a rose and the old saying is still true, that it is impossible to make a silk purse out of a sow's ear.

She must have had great artistic possibilities. But one thing is certain—she had no apparent means of promoting herself and had become discouraged trying. She came to me all in a heap. Discouragement and despair had reduced her almost to a state of hopelessness. But she did have faith in the Invisible, a good old-fashioned, orthodox faith.Now, in reality, we have very little to add to such conviction, but it does need to be directed. I think this is the true meaning of the saying that "faith without works is dead." It was impossible to get her to immediately understand philosophical or metaphysical problems and I made no attempt to do this. After all, simple trusting faith is the greatest thing in life and why should we try to change anyone's religious convictions? Or to erect a new and strange altar of faith before the God others worship? Let each seek Reality in his own way and if he is sincere, simple and direct in his method, surely that Presence to which the very hairs of our heads are numbered, will honor his approach.

We can add that we should all "make known our requests with thanksgiving," because thanksgiving is recognition, it is acceptance. We can add that doubts should be mentally assailed and destroyed in order that faith may become proved. But I have discovered in twenty-five years practice that if a man's faith is sufficient for him to live by, everything is well with him for a spiritual viewpoint, be he Jew, Protestant or Catholic.

Therefore, I did not say to this young man.. "You must come to believe as I do and cross all your "t's" and dot your "i's" as those in my belief do." Knowing that each is justified in his own belief and that each must approach the great reality in his own individual way, I said to her 'Let us take this thought together. We will set him up on high because he hath known my name'. This thought had a definite meaning to both of us, we could unite on it, we could each agree with it. For each of us it symbolized the concept that we are surrounded by an Infinite Presence which responds to our confidence in It.

Now I could have gone into an elaborate explanation and told her that the very nature of this Law compelled It to respond by exact correspondence. I could have lectured to her on the Law of Cause and Effect, on the principle of reflection or polarity. I could have expounded the theory of involution and evolution to her, all of which would have had no meaning whatsoever at that time, although it did come to have a meaning later. I merely said to her "Let us take this thought: 'I will set him up on high because he hath known my name'." I told her that we would try to feel that this had a very definite meaning in her experience for setting her up on high in her profession; meant that newspapers and billboards throughout the country and all over the world would some day carry her name in a prominent position.

Again we must remember that it is not the exact words we use so much as it is the meaning which these words convey to us which furnishes the power of spiritual mind treatments. In a most simple and childlike way, with all of the complete mental abandonment of trust and faith, she repeated these words after me: "I will set him up on high because he hath known my name."

Then I told her to practice the habit of mentally seeing herself as she would like to be; to definitely stop identifying herself with failure, to know that every doorway of opportunity was open to her, and to believe that every talent and ability which she possessed would be gladly recognized, welcomed, used and properly compensated for. I was able to formulate a very good and effective treatment using the simple thought, "I will set him up on high because he hath known my name."

It worked like a charm. There was nothing in her which denied what she was affirming. Everything within her accepted it with gratitude, with a joyous expectancy and this is exactly the attitude of thought we should have. We must believe, as Jesus said, that when we make known our requests we already receive the answer. I have never known anyone who, in a more simple, beautiful and direct way, believed. In fact, I used to marvel at her faith and I used to say, "are you quite sure that you know there is a Power which will go before you and prepare the way?" "Oh yes," she would say, "I have always believed in God."

"Well," I used to reply, "just keep right on. Use all the faith you have, intensify it with all the imagination and feeling you have, but never let go of this form of conviction. Take your thought and stay with it. 'I will set him up on high because he hath known my name.' And every time you use this statement, see yourself as you would like to be."

Nothing much happened for a few months, but gradually the doors opened. The gates stood ajar. The opportunity presented itself and she made good. I have no doubt that most of you who read this have seen her many times, for she is a wonderful artist.

He Knew More About Money Than He Did About Mind

He was a banker. Both his wife and daughter had received great benefits from attending our classes at the Institute and each hadreceived adequate proof that the Principle of Mind works for whomever accepts It. But he was a banker, understanding finance, good, solid business principles, conservative methods and orthodox ways of doing things. He was good, kindly and just, but I will have to confess that he lacked imagination.

Imagination is the spice of life. It is the pigment in the color. It is that without which things become rather drear and drab. I couldn't imagine a man spending his whole life just figuring out how much money he was going to make but, of course, we all realize the necessity of practical affairs in well-ordered lives. But to work only for the meat which perisheth is not to drink from that fountain of life which wells up from some source which is subterranean in our own natures.

I think this man never had drunk from this source. At any rate, he sat down with a sort of grunt, saying that while he must admit that his wife and daughter had received great benefit, and he was very grateful that they had, nevertheless he was a very practical man. He even admitted that he was unusually clever. My only remark was "Yeah?"

He began to tell me he had always been a great thinker, even profound. I couldn't help it, but again I said, "Yeah?" He took the attitude of "Show me if you dare." Now sometimes when people come to us with this attitude we are not interested in them. I have never liked to talk with people who kept saying, "Do you follow me?" "Do you get me?" or "If you understand what I mean."

I was talking with a man just recently who kept saying, "Do you follow me?" and after he had made this crack about the third time, I said, "Mister, I not only follow you but I am about two blocks down the road waiting for you to catch up. Please hurry." There are different kinds of smartness in this world. There is what we call gutter-smart. From a spiritual viewpoint it functions on a level little lower than that of the one who had intellectual arrogance. Intellectual arrogance amounts to spiritual stupidity. Be that as it may, I told the man that, quite contrary to his fond opinion of himself, my idea was that he had never really thought in his life. He had only imagined that he was thinking.

"But," he said, "I am a practical man. I deal with objective conditions and situations. I deal with practical affairs of life. I don't believe in mystery stuff." Naturally, I asked him what he considered the Life Principle to be anyway. At once he was on a raft in the middle of an ocean with neither sail, rudder nor anchor. I knew he would be. After which I proceeded to lay down the law to him, kindly but firmly. He was combative, aggressive, stupidly egotistical, but it was all to cover up an inward sensitivity. He was smart, clever, aggressive, but he lacked wisdom. Inwardly he was a child, hurt, rebuffed, distraught, uncertain. He lacked spiritual anchorage. His boat leaked and he didn't know how to repair it. He was sinking but hated to admit it. He stupidly put the telescope to his blind eye and exclaimed that he didn't see the signal.

He had bad stomach trouble. What a perfect, correspondent to his mental state. The funny thing about this man was that he took everything I had to say like a lamb and at the end of an hour's conversation he admitted that he really never had thought anything through. Practical, yes. Able to make a good living, most certainly. Well disposed toward humanity, without any doubt. Kindly and just. But the fountain of life was dried up at the source, ideas really didn't assimilate. I had to make him become childlike if he were to receive a new influx. There is no other way.

I compelled him to lay down before the altar of a new faith the entire body of his arrogance, to surrender the secret fears of his soul, and to come mentally clean before a new universe. I treated to know that the stomach is a divine instrument forever assimilating the ideas of harmony, of peace and of joy. I treated to know that his whole consciousness was open to the Divine influx. I worked to know that there was no sensitiveness, nothing to cover up, nothing to hide. The peace of God I realized to be at the center of his being.

His stomach ulcers disappeared and the natural processes of assimilation and elimination were restored to their proper activity. He became an enthusiastic, not "follower" for we dislike the term, but an enthusiastic believer in the Divine within every man. I am sure his whole life was changed.

We never consider physical healing of primal importance. If that comes, we should be very grateful, but we should recognize it merely as a sign following a new belief, a new outlook a new faith in life. What we call demonstration is an effect and not a cause, therefore it naturally follows that if one's consciousness becomes imbued with a greater degree of love, of understanding, of tolerance and of faith, his whole physical being will reflect this new mental state. This is how it is that physical healings are brought about.

Holmes' Advice On How To Treat

Holmes expected ministers of Religious Science to be adept at Treatment and to make it a part of their daily spiritual practice. If a minister came to him with a problem his first question was, "Have you been doing your treatment work?" If the answer was 'yes', he would then say, "We will do a treatment together now." Holmes wanted his ministers and practitioners to reach a sufficiently advanced level so that they could treat not only for others, but for themselves as well. He wanted them, according to Vetura Papke, "to learn to depend on God, not on another human being."

Holmes had many suggestions for those who wanted to perfect their skills as spiritual mind practitioners. There were steps which might be taken to increase chances of success and pitfalls which should be known about and avoided.

First and most important, the spiritual mind healer "must learn to see God in the patient and greet the Divinity in everyone." No matter what the objective appearance to the contrary might be, a practitioner should recognize that "a human being is still an eternal and perfect manifestation of the Divine." Holmes stressed the importance of the practitioner's ability to see harmony instead of discord, and to keep unified with the Divine Presence. The most important thing anyone can learn, he reiterated, "is that there is a Presence and a Power to which we may turn, which will always turn to us as we turn to it, which will always meet our needs if we believe. This is the essence of our faith."

Holmes advised that every statement in a treatment should be clear cut and positive. "It should arrive from the consciousness that good is the only power that is." It was important that the practitioner "always expect the good," and above all, "have a consciousness of love—a radiant feeling flowing through your consciousness at all times." Holmes saw the effective practitioner as a "master electrician," as one who "knows the power they are dealing with and how to use it."

It was essential for practitioners to have "confidence in the Law." The effective practitioner in this science, said Holmes, "has the will to try, the courage to make the attempt and the faith to believe in himself." Belief was vitally needed. It was not the words used in treatment that made the difference, Holmes pointed out, but what one believes. In fact treatments need not be long-winded or wordy. Treatments were effective only because of the meaning attached to the words. "It was always out of the fire of the heart," he said, "that the mouth must speak."

A basic tenet of our "metaphysical technique" in formulating treatments, said Holmes, "was simply knowing the truth about people, and not wondering how it is going to reach them or when it will. . . . Listening to the Divine Presence, desiring only that which is right, the practitioner of spiritual mind science must know that he is using a Law of cause and effect which is immutable."

Holmes taught that it was the practitioner's primary job to "untangle the wrong thoughts through the recognition of the Omnipresence of God or Truth." Treatment, he pointed out, "deals with thought rather than people." From the standpoint of the mental practitioner, "disease must be seen as. . . . a mental declaration of discord, an argument of confusion, or a mental expression of negation." It was essential that the practitioner view the patient's condition, "no matter what

the condition is and no matter what it is pronounced to be, "as a thing of thought." If it was viewed in any other way, it would be impossible to treat. "If it is not thought," Holmes pointed out, "how is thought going to reach it?" This was a critical point in mental healing, said Holmes, "for unless the practitioner of the science could resolve things into thoughts he would have no mental method or procedure which would sound reasonable, sane or scientific." Unless disease "originates in consciousness",
Holmes observed, "consciousness cannot change it."

The thought that the practitioner focused on and dealt with was not that of the client. It was the practitioner's own thinking that was at issue. Nothing was done to the client. No personal influence was attempted. "The work begins and ends," said Holmes, "in the thought of the one giving treatment." The practitioner must do the work within oneself, and realize "in his own mind" the truth about the person. "The practitioner treats the practitioner, for the patient, always. . . . The practitioner never tries to get away from the mind within." The practitioner's work consists, said Holmes, "in reversing the negative thought in his own mind."

The practitioner goes about the work by making statements about the client that, according to Holmes, "tend to clear up, in his own thought, his belief about the person for whom he is treating." This work continues until the practitioner finally comes to a place where there is an inner knowing that the person is healed and free from the condition. Holmes spoke of his own experience as a practitioner and described how he did it. "I keep working on myself to bring the mind to a place where it finally accepts that there is a Universal Principle acting through Law."

Treatment works better if the practitioner expects immediate success. "You should always expect instantaneous and permanent results." If you do not, Holmes warned, "you cannot attain them." Expectancy, he said, "speeds progress." You should always live in "continual state of expectancy."

Practitioners should not end the treatment until they feel certain that all has been done that needs doing. Before ending the treatment, the Practitioner "should feel it is Complete and Perfect, that it is finished and done." Treatment is not complete, Holmes said, until the practitioner "in his own consciousness, accepts the verdict as Final and Perfect."

Holmes believed that daily meditation facilitated practitioners in their work. Every practitioner, he advised, "should take a certain time every day to meditate within himself, to realize that the words which he speaks are the words of truth." Holmes recognized that learning to meditate took practice. "It is not done overnight," he said, so he urged practitioners, "each day, without fail, to give time to meditation. Sit quietly, forget everything that suggests chaotic conditions or personal dilemmas. Each time negative thought presents itself to your mind you discard it from your mind. Do not be discouraged if at first your mind seems to wander. Persistently put every diverse thought out of your mind until you have forged the habit of controlling your own mental action."

There were many pitfalls to be avoided in the practice of Treatment. The use of will power was one of them. Will power should never be used in treatment, Holmes advised. "Too much cannot be said against the belief that will power is creative." Under no circumstances should will power be used to force change to happen. Any idea of using will power to influence people, said Holmes, "is a mistake." Holmes also warned that the practitioner does not "suggest, hypnotize, or mentally influence." All that is necessary is to know that the person is a spiritual being.

Holmes recognized that in performing treatment the practitioner must be careful, because it was possible to make the problem worse, to perpetuate the difficulty rather than resolve it. "Too often," he said, "our treatments are really new ways of stating our fears, new ways of affirming our negations. Somewhere in the treatment the mind must swing

clear from the negation, clear from the negative affirmation.
. . . We must be very careful indeed in using our denials of
evil that they do not really terminate in affirmations of evil,
for this one could do very easily. In other words, he warned,
"don't fight the devil so hard that you create him out of your
own mental struggle and combat."

Holmes warned against "hoping treatment would work."
When a practitioner treats, said Holmes, he or she "does not
just hope that the patient will get well," and does not ask that
the patient be healed. "Watch yourselves very carefully when
you treat," he advised, "and be sure that your treatment is
not merely a mental wishing," or not simply "wistful day-
dreaming."

Holmes cautioned against "passive" treatments, ones in
which no definite statement of intention or want is declared.
"If we give treatments without a definite motive in mind, the
most we can accomplish will be to promote a salutary atmosphere." A passive meditation, he noted, "will never produce an active demonstration."

Fear and doubt are other major pitfalls for a practitioner. "Fear," he once said, "is the greatest enemy of man." A
practitioner is continually confronted, he lamented, "with
the fog of fear, superstition and doubt." Failure to deal with
these difficulties destroys the practitioner's effectiveness.
"Either he will get lost in the fog," said Holmes, "or see
through it. Though the fog is there, the sun is always shining.
This is what he clings to."

Holmes felt strongly that treatment should not be considered difficult or hard. "When we know that there is but
one mind, we shall realize that the work could not be difficult
or laborious. It would be a mistake to work in any other than
a calm, peaceful way. Treatment should never be done with
a sense of morbidity or struggle, or in any sense that we are
fighting opposing forces, but rather, with a calm, peaceful
inward assurance."

When asked whether it was possible for treatment to fail, Holmes replied, "There are no failures." A failure was merely "our present inability to measure up. . . . The Spirit cannot fail. What we call a failure is merely a limited way in which we are using a limitless Principle." If the practitioner entertains the idea that he or she failed, that idea should be completely erased from the mind. If one believes "that he failed last year," said Holmes, "he will likely fail again this year, unless that false thought is erased." False thought was always something to be guarded against. Someone once asked him, "Dr. Holmes, how do you heal someone of illness?" Holmes replied, "What is there to heal?"

Holmes warned that a treatment would fail if a practitioner assumed personal responsibility for its outcome. "Do not feel you must heal anyone," Holmes told his practitioners. "Every sense of personal responsibility and individual obligation, other than to do one's work to the best of one's ability must be dropped from the mind. The practitioner should never feel anxiety about the outcome. Holmes advised, "Never let one moment's responsibility rest in your own thought about it." The only duty the practitioner had was "to set the Law in motion." The responsibility for making it work was inherent in the nature of the Law of Mind itself.

Holmes advised his practitioners that it was not necessary for patients to be in their presence for treatment to work. "There is no difference," he said, "between absent and present treatment." The practitioner need only to know who is to be helped and for what problem. It was not necessary for the practitioner to know where the person was or what the person was doing during treatment.

While Holmes believed it important that the patient "be willing to give up anything and everything that would hinder the demonstration," he advised his practitioners that the patient's cooperation and consent was not essential to the success of the treatment. "When you treat a person," Holmes said, "you are merely recognizing him as a spiritual being now." That was all that was necessary. Whether or not you had the person's consent made no difference.

Holmes put the essence of his teaching about Spiritual Mind Treatment in the following statement. He said, "Since all creation is mental, it follows that if all things are created by the Mind of God, and man's mind is a part of God's Mind, man is able, by thinking, to set in motion a power that creates. . . . We need, therefore, only to clear our minds of unbelief, and know that it is done unto us as we believe. In this spirit we can think thoughts of success, and success will follow as surely as night follows day."

Holmes did not believe in proselytizing. "It was not necessary," he told his ministers and practitioners, "for us to always be running around telling how wonderful our truth is and trying to persuade others to believe as we do." In fact, he said, "it isn't at all desirable." Holmes believed that the important thing was to live the teaching. "First, last, and all the time," he said, "our whole process is demonstration. . . . What we need to do is to demonstrate that spiritual thought force is a dynamic reality in human experience. . . . It is the demonstrating of greater peace in our lives, a greater joy in our own consciousness, a greater spontaneity in our whole expression, and a fuller, more successful and more vital life."

Holmes felt that others would believe without being told. "Let us practice our belief in our own interior," he said, "until other people see in our daily living the outward result of our inner belief and conviction." It was important to Holmes, not to try to make converts. "Under no circumstance," he warned, "should this attempt be made."

Practicing Spiritual Mind Treatment For Yourself

While Holmes focused primarily upon how a Spiritual Mind Practitioner would treat for others, he did not ignore or deny the importance of individuals gaining the ability to

treat for themselves. He made it clear that professional practitioners, before they were ready to treat for others, had to be
able to work for themselves. "We must use the power to help
ourselves first," he said, "in order that we may establish a
realization of our ability to use it for others."

Holmes urged professional practitioners to teach their
clients to treat for themselves. "One of the problems that
confronts a practitioner," said Holmes, was how to free the
client "from the bondage of continually turning to external
aid." Clients needed to stand on their own two feet and wean
themselves away from the practitioner. Holmes told practitioners that it was their duty to facilitate their clients in
learning "to use the Law" for themselves. The client must
arrive at a point where "he knows that he is rooted in pure
Spirit, and that his own word is the law of his own being."

Holmes advised people to practice Spiritual Mind Treatment on a daily basis. The formal method he recommended
was simple and easy to do. "Take a definite time, at least
twice each day to be alone," he said. One should "sit down,
compose your mind and think about God. Try to arrive at a
deep sense of peace and calm, a faith in a Power greater than
you are. Say: 'The words I speak are the Law of God.' Next
say, 'My body is a manifestation of the Living Spirit.' Next
deny everything that contradicts this. (You now have reached
a place of realization which you enter into a feeling of assurance.) Then say, "It is now done. It is now complete.'"

Holmes commented on the benefits to individuals of
being able to treat without the aid of a professional practitioner. "It is wonderful to realize that we can sit in the quiet of
our own being and consciously direct a power greater than
we are for the definite purpose of helping ourselves."

Holmes viewed it as an ideal of human spiritual ad-
vancement if a person could at all times maintain the mind
state achieved during treatment. It was his hope that in their
daily lives people could learn to "continually maintain an
attitude and frame of mind that embodies spiritual mind

treatment." While he knew this was a lofty ideal, one that most people were unable to attain, he was clear in his own mind that human beings needed to be more connected with the spirit within. He once commented, "We have become technologized, we are modernized, we are industrialized, we are commercialized, and in the last 25 years we have been psychologized. But who can say that we are civilized? We shall never become civilized until we first become spiritualized."

Positive Thought

While Spiritual Mind Treatment is the primary spiritual tool of the philosophy of Science of Mind, Holmes acknowledged that it was not always necessary to go through all the steps of treatment to prevent negative thinking from dominating consciousness. Holmes believed that in many circumstances negative thought could be dissipated through strict censorship over the mind. "Just as you watch your garden so that foreign seeds shall not fall into it, producing a growth of undesirable plants, so you must refuse entrance to any thoughts you do not wish to see manifested in your life."

Thinking positively was one method and it could be done by choice. "We should decide to think on the affirmative side of life," he said, "We will be pleased with the results. In such degree as your thought has a preponderance of successful feeling your living will become successful." In one of his earliest writings (1919) he made the point with great emphasis. He assured his readers, "The man who can control his thought can have and do what he wishes to have and to do. Everything is his for the asking."

Holmes believed that "thoughts are things." That which existed on the subjective side of life would ultimately manifest on the material side. "The greatest discovery man has ever made," he said, "was that thought has creative power." We could control our affairs "by right thinking," and by so doing bring into our experience the things we wished to enjoy. He therefore advised, "If you don't like the effects you've been getting in your life, change the cause."

The use of affirmations was one important way of changing the cause. "No matter how subtle the thoughts of lack, fear, uncertainty or loneliness may be," he said, "your affirmations can erase them." He recommended that one should "keep knocking at the doorway of consciousness until every 'no' becomes a 'yes,' every negative an affirmative, every fear a faith."

When a person was plagued by negative thoughts, and "became discouraged and mentally depressed," Holmes suggested the following approach: Sit in "quiet contemplation for a few moments." It is likely, he predicted, that one would become so stilled that the "Spirit of Divine Reality" would dissipate the negation. The depressed state of mind might "disappear as mist before the sun."

If this foreshortened approach failed it was then appropriate to take the time to go through each of the steps of Spiritual Mind Treatment or seek help from a practitioner.

CHAPTER III

I Didn't Make It Up

Influences

Ernest Holmes was a synthesizer of the work of others rather than a creator of a new philosophical system. "It all came from somewhere," he said. "I didn't make it up. The thing that is original about us is that we don't claim any originality." Holmes credited his many years of private study of spiritual teachings as being responsible for the development of his philosophical ideas. "Religious Science and Science of Mind," he said, "came into being, not as something better than any one of them, but rather as a synthesis of all of them."

In creating Science of Mind, Holmes attempted to bring "the great philosophical and spiritual truths" into line with "the modern metaphysical knowledge of the law of mind in action." While these ideas had been advanced before, what was new, he suggested, "is the approach to these ideas and the way in which they can be used in practical down-to-earth every day living."

Arthur Vergara, an editor with DeVorss & Company, the long-time metaphysical publishing company in Los Angeles, and author of a forth-coming book on New Thought teaching, agreed with Holmes' own assessment of his contribution. Vergara viewed Holmes as "a synthesizer, popularizer and simplifier.... The whole idea of treatment was on the scene before Holmes arrived," said

Vergara. Holmes found out what was successful in all the other systems, "what really worked." His contribution was to "simplify it, refine it, divest it of superstition, and give it an actual sequence of steps."

The principal ideas that Holmes advanced in the Science of Mind were taken from the writings of late 19th century and early twentieth century thinkers whose philosophical teachings came to be known as "New Thought." Robert E. Ellwood, author of *Religious and Spiritual Groups in Modern America* stated that the roots of New Thought were in the German idealism of George Friedrich Hegel and the New England Transcendentalism of Ralph Waldo Emerson. New Thought, said Ellwood, "was a modern western adaptation of the assumption that mind is fundamental and causative." Its major proponents, in addition to Holmes, were Phineas Quimby, Ralph Waldo Trine and Horatio Dresser in the United States, and Thomas Troward in England.

All sought to show how thoughts of health, wholeness, and success created their corresponding material realities. Since the inner reality of the universe is mind and ideas, they postulated that people, by changing their thought, could change the physical world. Special emphasis was always put on healing, both of mind and body. New Thought shared a basic presupposition with two other late nineteenth century philosophical movements, Spiritualism and Theosophy, which viewed the mind as sovereign and capable of transcending all limitations the world seems to place around it.

Holmes acknowledged his debt to Phineas P. Quimby, the watchmaker from Belfast, Maine, whose *Quimby Manuscripts,* Holmes said, "constitute a compilation of the most original sayings in one book that were ever uttered by the mind of man." What was so revolutionary in Quimby, said Holmes, was "his belief that all disease is a result of the misuse of the Mind Principle." While Quimby saw the "perfection at the center of everything," he did not, Holmes noted, "reduce this theory to a definite concept that could be practiced."

Thomas Troward, the English jurist, metaphysician and author of *The Edinburgh Lectures on Mental Science,* was another major influence. "I consider Troward's writings to be the most profound spiritual abstractions of modern times," said Holmes. But like Quimby, Holmes recognized that Troward "taught very little about the application of his belief to practical matters." In many of Holmes' articles, books and lectures he quoted at length from Troward. "I would say," Holmes once recalled, "that 25% of our philosophy comes from Troward."

The work of Mary Baker Eddy and the Christian Science movement was also another major influence. Holmes' introduction to mental healing was at the Mother Church in Boston when he was a young man. Robert Bitzer, one of Holmes' earliest associates, who knew Holmes well in the 1920s, recalls that Holmes knew by heart Mary Baker Eddy's textbook on Christian Science, *Science and Health,* and could quote at length from it.

Although Holmes was never a member of the Christian Science movement, Bitzer reports that at one time the shingle outside Holmes practitioner office read, "Ernest Holmes, Christian Science Practitioner." Bitzer said that Holmes "never lost his respect for Mrs. Eddy and his love for her teaching." Bitzer believes that Mrs. Eddy "had a great influence in his work."

In 1924 Holmes sought out Emma Curtis Hopkins, a renowned teacher of many leaders of the New Thought movement, and author of the widely respected book *High Mysticism.* "I was fortunate," Holmes later said, "to have been able to take her lessons on mysticism." Though only twelve lessons in all, each one hour long, the work with Mrs. Hopkins had an important impact. "She had a transcendence about her," Holmes recalled, "that you could feel. It was really there. . . . she was an illumined soul."

A major influence at a critical early point in his life was Ralph Waldo Emerson, the early 19th century American Transcendentalist and author of a classic series of essays. Emerson taught that the highest revelation of God to man lies within man himself. This approach had an early appeal to Holmes. "When I was a kid I began studying Emerson," Holmes recalled. "I have studied Emerson all my life." Holmes continually mentioned Emerson with Jesus and the Buddha as being, in his estimation, among the world's most enlightened human beings.

Holmes was a dedicated reader of sacred scripture. The Bible was a book that was always at his bedside. He read it with regularity throughout his lifetime. While the teachings of Christian religion did not appeal to him, the teachings of Jesus, as he interpreted them from his reading of the Bible, had a major import.[1]

Holmes spoke of Jesus in exalted terms. He called Jesus, "the most glorious soul who ever trod our planet," "the most tremendous example of the possibility of man," "a way shower of truth and life," "the most profound philosopher who ever lived," "a consciously cosmic soul," "the one who spoke as never before." Jesus stood alone, Holmes said, "as a man who knew himself and realized his relationship to the Perfect Whole." The birth of Jesus, Holmes said, "was undoubtedly the greatest historical event in the history of the human race."

Holmes attributed the greatness of Jesus to his knowledge of spiritual truth and his experience of himself as one with God. "Jesus sensed the Divine Presence in the most intimate manner possible," said Holmes. "He lived in such close communion with the Spirit that his words were always a reflection of the Pattern...All of his parables rest on the fundamental conception of the unity of God with man, the oneness of all life and the necessity of our coming into conscious recognition of our divine nature."

Holmes saw Jesus as "The Great Revelator," as the one "who laid down the rules for the game of life. He had found the keys to the Kingdom of Heaven. He had unlocked the door and entered. He had found the light."

Holmes made a clear distinction between "Jesus" and "Christ". "Jesus," he said, "is the name of a man," while Christ was "the Universal Principle of Divine Sonship, the generic man, the Divine Pattern, the ideal toward which humanity evolves, the apex of individual evolution, the conscious union of God and Man." Holmes wanted to make it clear that Christ represented the "universal possibility" for all men. "I want to think of Christ," he said, "not as a person, but as an active Principle of Intelligence in the Universe." Every man is "a potential Christ, from the least to the greatest; the same life runs through us all, threading itself into the patterns of our individuality."

Holmes believed that Jesus himself, during his lifetime, increasingly perceived his own personal relationship with the Christ principle inherent in all people. By the time he died, Holmes thinks that he did in fact become "Jesus the Christ". Holmes set forth his own views on Christianity's claims for Jesus' divinity when he said, "Mental science does not deny the divinity of Jesus, but it does affirm the divinity of all people. It does not deny that Jesus was the Son of God, but it affirms that all men are the sons of God. It does not deny that the kingdom of God was revealed through Jesus, but it says that the Kingdom of God is also revealed through you and me."

Holmes asserted that Christianity misinterpreted the teachings of Jesus and tried to make him "the great exception" instead of "the great example". Holmes did not criticize Christianity for lack of sincerity in its desire to follow its great teacher. "The great mistake," he said, was in "a misconception of his message." Holmes thought the problem lay in Christianity's literal interpretation of the Biblical message. "If the life and message and work of Jesus," Holmes said, "was to be taken with an absolute literal meaning, then in a way, the unique form of Jesus would become God, and unfortunately would lose for us the perspective of the most tremendous example of the possibility of man."

Holmes asserted that Jesus did not attempt to set himself up as God to be prayed to or worshipped. "It is high time," Holmes demanded, "that we learn the obvious fact that when Jesus referred to himself as the Son of God he was not trying to set himself apart from other men. What he was trying to do was reveal to the people of his day that they too were sharers of the Divine Nature."

Holmes saw the mission of Jesus and that of the prophet Moses as being related. Moses taught the universal law of cause and effect and Jesus applied it to human relations. "It was the mission of Jesus to add beauty to the power, to put feeling to that which itself is merely a mechanical law." Holmes concluded that Jesus stressed two basic principles: that Christ is the revelation of God to man, the Incarnation of the Divine in the human, and that man's true nature is divine and therefore everyone is a center for the activity of the consciousness of God.

Given Holmes' interpretation of the teachings of Jesus on the nature of God, it is not surprising that he saw the miracles of Jesus as examples of spiritual mind healing. "The so-called miracles of Jesus," Holmes asserted, "were logical outcomes of his spiritual wisdom. They were not miracles at all but mathematical manifestations of the creative power of a man's thought."

In Holmes' view, Jesus addressed the problems of disease and human suffering in the same way a Religious Science practitioner would deal with it in Spiritual Mind Treatment. "Recognizing his unity with God," Holmes observed, Jesus "met every form of disease and every discordant circumstance and changed it by a word. He refused to believe that discord was the ultimate reality. He refused to believe that evil had any place in the Kingdom of Heaven."

Holmes asserted that Jesus understood the essence of treatment and used it effectively. "I believe," said Holmes, "that his consciousness of the word he spoke was followed by immediate right action because he expected it to be. It seems to me that when Jesus said, 'take up thy bed and walk,' his inner thought accepted the fact that the man would take up his bed and walk." Jesus announced the Law of the Mind, Holmes observed, when he said, "It is done unto you as you believe."

While Holmes felt the principle of Spiritual Mind Treatment was implied in several passages of the Bible, he acknowledged that the technique was never fully explained. "One would never learn how to give an effective mental treatment by studying it," Holmes observed. "We would no more learn how to give a treatment by studying the Bible than we could learn how to psychoanalyze a person."

Holmes saw a close relationship between the teachings of Jesus and his own philosophy of Science and Mind. "In the record of his sayings," Holmes argued, "there is much that bears witness to our own belief, and no doubt could we penetrate completely into the meaning of his teachings, we would have a perfect explanation for our own philosophy."

Modern Psychology

Holmes was intrigued by the findings of the emerging field of psychology. His articles in *Science of Mind* magazine throughout the 1930s and 1940s are filled with references, both to psychological studies which shed light on the problems of human existence, and to the works of the leading figures in the field including Freud, Adler, Jung and William James.[2]

The new information facilitated his own work. "Much of the new psychology," he said, "contributes to the practice of Science of Mind." He acknowledged that "psychology has chartered the subconscious and defined many of the inhibiting facts that are behind the average sickness, unhappiness and failure to have a full and constructive life." Psychology had proved, he said, "that it is not the experience we have that hurts us, but our emotional reaction to the experience. . . . that nine tenths of our reactions are subconscious. . . . that by far the largest portion of consciousness is submerged. . . that our conscious actions are definitely influenced by this unconscious field of thought"

The greatest weakness he observed in the field of psychology was its underlying materialism. It neglected the spiritual. He foresaw no possibility for psychology to accomplish lasting results "without returning to some form of spiritual conviction."

Holmes was particularly attracted to the work of Carl Jung. He was pleased that Jung acknowledged the role of the spiritual in the life of humankind. During his thirty five years of experience as a psychologist, Jung had observed (according to Holmes) that he (Jung) had never known an absolute healing without the restoration of faith. Holmes was pleased that Jung had discovered that people without belief in their own spiritual nature were not nearly as happy in their advancing years as those "who have a satisfactory spiritual conviction."

PSI Phenomena

Holmes was interested in any subject which provided useful information on the operation of the human mind. Early in his career he recognized the importance of understanding PSI phenomena. Without a thorough acquaintance with it, he said, "we do not understand the complete workings of the mind. We do not understand the experiences people often have, and in a consistent philosophy which deals with the mind, the lack of understanding of psychic phenomena would be inexcusable."[3]

When Holmes published the first edition of his text *Science of Mind* in 1928 he had become convinced that human beings, through some power "independent of the body", can "see, hear, feel, smell, touch and taste without the aid of the physical instrument". He concluded that "psychic phenomena are caused by some mental power." Of that, he said, "there can be no doubt." People with well-developed psychic abilities could see mental pictures clairvoyantly, "and read our thoughts telepathically".

A good medium, he observed, "had the ability, more or less clearly, to bring these pictures and thoughts to the surface and objectify them". Everyone leaves behind mental pictures of themselves, he believed, and "anyone who had developed their psychic abilities had access to these images. . . . A psychic going into more or less of a subjective state is able to enter into the vibration of an individual's thought and read from the book of remembrance. . . . In certain psychic states people can see, hear, and read others thoughts, travel abroad, and perform many other marvelous feats, which in the conscious state are impossible".

Holmes spoke of his own ability to "hear the inner voice speak," and obtain information through clairvoyance. "Such voices do speak," he said, "and they are real. I have heard animated and interesting conversations with such voices for hours at a sitting, and it has been a wonderful experience." Though he had difficulty determining the exact nature of psychic phenomena, he was sure of the fact that "the phenomena transpires, as wonderful messages come through in this manner."

In the 1930s Holmes grew to doubt the value of psychic information. He concluded that the inappropriate use of psychic powers could impede spiritual growth. In the October 1934 issue of *Science of Mind* magazine he stated, "The world has always had great psychics, and always will have, and always needs them. But we must stop and see where their advice comes from. We cannot blindly believe something just because someone in a trance tells us it is so. We must say, 'Does it work? Is it intelligent?'"

Holmes had begun to distinguish information that came through psychically from that which he believed had a mystical origin. "We have had great mystics in the world, great spiritual geniuses like Jesus, great spiritual men like Emerson, and hundreds of others. Not one of these people was psychically confused." These people, Holmes said, "had plunged not only beneath the material surface, but also through the psychic confusion of the race mind into that rarefied atmosphere, into that purified consciousness, that eternal and perfect reality which is God."

Holmes had come to believe that some psychics, functioning in a trance state, "get messages from beyond that are garbled and confused." In some cases people became possessed by a spirit which puts them into "a sort of psychic frenzy, a subtle insanity which is not to be considered at all in the light of spiritual illumination or Divine Reality."

Holmes felt that part of the problem lay in the fact that many psychics, in order to get information, had to go into the trance state. He felt that such states of consciousness were abnormal and potentially dangerous. "Any state bordering on trance or hypnotism through self suggestion is far removed from the field of reality where the consciousness should be aware." He was concerned in part because he believed that people in states of trance might become possessed "by discarnate spirits, earth bound elementals" and other harmful forces.

In the second edition of the textbook on *Science of Mind* Holmes omitted most of the material contained in the first edition on psychic laws and psychism. It appears that he had concluded that it was an area which was too wrought with misunderstanding and misinformation. He was also concerned that some of his spiritual mind practitioners were incorporating psychic readings into their treatments. This was an abuse of his teachings. "Occult and esoteric practices," he wrote, "are neither necessary nor beneficial in this work."

Despite his reservations, Holmes maintained an interest in the subject. He kept up a personal relationship with one of the most renowned psychics of the time, Eileen Garrett, and acquainted himself with the work of J. B. Rhine, the Duke University professor who in the 1930s founded a major psychic research lab. By the 1950s Holmes seemed more open to the possibilities that were now presenting themselves. In an article in *Science of Mind* magazine in 1951 he commented that the experiments that Dr. Rhine had been conducting for the past twenty years had proved the existence of extra sensory perception (ESP) and supra normal powers. "In his experiments," Holmes commented, "he has demonstrated that we can produce the activities of the five senses without using the sense organs". Holmes concluded that Rhine's experiments were a new and important advance. "If such things can be done in a psychological laboratory," Holmes surmised, "why should we doubt that transcendent power of the Spirit." Holmes saw Rhine's work as providing evidence "of an inner self that you and I did not put there, an inner self with forces and powers that are transcendent of our ordinary experiences".

Given Holmes' strong belief in the benefits of his own teaching regarding healing, one might suspect that he would take a dim view of the benefits of other forms, particularly that of the medical professions. Such was not the case. He had a great respect for modern medicine. "The world needs all the help it can receive from any source," he said, "We do not deny that people are ill or that they need healing. We do not deny the reality of physical or psychological aid." The metaphysician, he said, "will cooperate with doctors, social workers, psychologists or any other group of people who are seeking to alleviate human distress. To refuse to do so would be both ignorant and superstitious."

He recalled that, in the early days of "spiritual therapeutics" (another term for spiritual mind treatment), it was believed that one could not mentally treat people with success if they were being treated by physicians, or if they were using material methods (medicine) for relief. "We now know that idea was based on superstition. We no longer give it serious thought."

Holmes had come to believe that treatment worked better when the patient was getting proper physical care. "There is an added comfort in the mind of the patient when he knows he is having proper physical care, proper diet, right medical and surgical attention, if necessary. His mind is in a more composed state. Being less disturbed the mental practitioner can do more effective work for him."

Holmes felt that great benefit would accrue to society when doctors, psychologists and metaphysicians better understood each other's contribution, and cooperated working with clients and patients. "It is self-evident," he stated, "that each is seeking to alleviate human suffering." While it would be foolish to deny the contribution of the medical profession, he observed, "it was generally agreed that a large percentage of our physical troubles are mental in origin, and that all have some relationship to mental processes." He felt it important that the medical profession, "both understand and appreciate the work of the sincere metaphysicians."

CHAPTER IV

He Conveyed Something More Than Could Be Said In Words

Lf there was one place where Ernest Holmes felt absolutely at home, it was on a speaker's platform. The testimony of person after person on his impact as an inspirational speaker indicates that before an audience of people Ernest Holmes had few equals. The following observations by people who were either personal friends or professional associates provide an idea of his extraordinary ability.[1]

Elaine St. Johns: "Ernest on the platform was charged with an enormous spiritual energy. It didn't make any difference what he said, something came out that was catalytic and synergetic."

David Bushness: "When he spoke, it was as though the message was being spoken through him. It would just flow out. Sometimes when he stopped, he'd ask, 'Did I say that?' The message came through him so beautifully and so clear. He was a real channel, a conscious channel, tuned into the basic truths of the universe."

Fletcher Harding: "Ernest was the best speaker I ever heard. He was most effective at moving an audience, exciting and inspiring it."

William H. D. Hornaday: "When he taught he conveyed something more than could be said in words...Whether in the lecture hall or the classroom, people who heard him speak felt better afterwards, though they didn't entirely understand why."

Reginald Armor: "I asked a friend to describe the key point that Ernest brought out in his talk, and he replied in all seriousness, 'I really don't know. No, I really don't know much about what he said, but I sure did like it.'"

Vetura Papke: "He had that wonderful ability to create a feeling of ecstasy, and then drop you down with a laugh or a story. He was very down to earth, but inspiring. I heard all the great ministers of the time from Emmett Fox to the Fillmores and none of them compared to Ernest."

Bill Lynn: "Ernest often opened his lectures with the words, 'There is a power in the Universe and you can use it.' The impact of those words the first time I heard him, is something I will never forget. Shivers went down my spine. I couldn't believe the powerful voice that was coming out of that funny little man."

Frank Richelieu: "He had a gorgeous speaking voice and his timing was fabulous. He could draw you to the edge of your seat, because you thought he was speaking directly to you."

Jack Addington: "When you heard Ernest speak you heard a message that went deep into your soul. He had something solid to give you."

Carleton Whitehead: "Ernest was peerless on the platform. He captured the audience with his first sentence and maintained its rapt attention throughout. During the last ten minutes, as a musician raises pitch for emphasis, Dr. Holmes would magically infuse his message with a higher tone and give an incredible lift to his listeners."

Craig Carter: "In the last three or four years of his life Ernest rose to greater heights of spiritual inspiration than at any other time. The last years were the finest. It seemed the longer he went the better he got."[2]

Many believe that his last speech, given just two months before he died, at the dedication of the church in Whittier was his best. Elaine St. Johns remarked that in that speech he lived up to the words of his long-time idol, Ralph Waldo Emerson, who said, "What you *are* speaks so loudly that I cannot hear what you say." It was during that speech he suddenly paused and then was silent for a long time. He then said, "I am beyond words. I have no more words for you. It's here. It's here. It's here."

Given the extraordinary quality of his talks one might expect that Holmes spent large amounts of time preparing them. Such apparently is not the case. Elaine St. Johns reported that Holmes never knew beforehand what he was going to talk about. "The way he prepared for his talks was to water Hazel's succulents." While a member of the Holmes household, Bill Lynn, then only a teenager, observed Holmes' Sunday morning routine. "About an hour before he was to talk he would disappear into his study. And that hour was given to meditation and treatment. He never made notes, he never planned out a lecture, and he always spoke extemporaneously."

Holmes never wrote out a lecture, or as Reginald Armor noted, "read one that someone else had written for him." However, Holmes, in fact, observed Armor, "was always preparing." Early in the week he would begin to think about his speaking topic, "and while he would say, 'never prepare anything,' he would go up and down and ask people their opinions about various ideas on this particular subject churning in his mind all week long. So actually, he was not only prepared to speak, but he was constantly preparing."

When on the speaking platform Holmes believed, according to Lynn, that there was a spirit that spoke for him, an inner voice that he listened to as he spoke. "Don't listen to what you speak," he told Lynn, "but speak what you hear." Sometimes he marveled at what he himself had to say, acknowledging that the words had come from a source outside his own consciousness. On Monday mornings at the Institute in Los Angeles he would often ask the ministers there, "Did you make Big Talk yesterday?" Then he might answer for himself. "As a matter of fact I did make Big Talk yesterday. It was so good I could hardly wait to hear what I was going to say."

While he knew he was capable of remarkable things on the platform he was not pompous, did not put on airs or act superior. As Vetura Papke observed, "He never wanted us to feel that he was more important than anyone else." He loved humor, loved to joke. Jack Addington recalled that Holmes was a good laugher. "When he had something to laugh at he would *laugh*." Bill Lynn reported that his talks were filled with humor and he himself was often the butt of his own words. One Sunday morning after a particularly good talk he wrote the following doggerel. It shows how lightly he took himself as a speaker.

> *Talk, talk, talk, talk*
> *I Love its giddy gurgle*
> *I Love its fluent flow.*
> *I Love to wind my tongue up*
> *I Love to hear it go.*
> *I used to think I knew I knew,*
> *But now I must confess*
> *The more I know I know*
> *I know I know the less.*

Remarkable as he was on the speaker's platform his performance was not always flawless. On occasion he made a mis-step in a speech. Lynn noted that there were times when he got off track. Then he might stop and say to his audience. "Did you understand that? It's clear as mud to me." He'd then back up and start again. At other times he would sense that he was losing his audience. On these occasions he would pause, take out his handkerchief and blow his nose. "It was the biggest honk you ever heard," says Lynn. "It shocked a lot of people, but it woke up the audience, showed them that he was human, and provided him with a chance to shift gears."

Holmes was an avid reader, and during his talks he would recite passages from the Bible or from the poems of favorite authors. Since he did not speak from notes, it was often observed that, despite his excellent memory, he misquoted verses and even passages from sacred scripture. When it was brought to his attention, he would say, "The meaning and feeling generated are the important things," and then, with a twinkle would add, "Don't quote me on quotes."

Holmes had strong ideas on how the Sunday service should be conducted. Craig Carter reports that he believed that it was important for the minister to greet people as they arrived. It was equally important that he leave immediately after the service was over. "If I have done my job properly on the platform" he said, "the only appropriate thing for me to do at the end of my sermon is to disappear." If you had lifted people to sublime heights of spiritual realization, then standing around and chatting was not what you did. Reginald Armor recalled that Holmes believed that people attended Sunday service for teaching and inspiration, and not entertainment. The sermon was the key event.

The appearance of the platform and its adornment was also important to him. In the 1950s Jack Addington, then a Religious Science ministers in San Diego, invited Holmes to speak at his church. When he arrived the platform was decorated with flowers. He immediately ordered them to be removed. He told Addington, "When you are on the platform, you are the attraction. You are what they are there to hear. They didn't come to see flowers. And if you have someone else on the platform, they will detract from you. Never have anyone else on the platform with you, unless you can't avoid it. Keep the platform clear. The attraction is the speaker."

When he spoke on Sundays, William Hornaday recalls that he stood beside the podium rather than behind it. He did this because he wanted people to have a full view of him.

According to Elaine St. Johns, Holmes preferred speaking on Sunday mornings to an audience in a movie theater rather than preaching to a congregation in a church. All through his 30-year ministry he spoke in theaters in the Wilshire District, not far from downtown Los Angeles. Throughout his active ministry he never had a church of his own. One of the reasons may have been his preference for the unadorned speaking platforms and the non-church atmosphere of the movie theaters.

"Ernest was not a churchman," Fletcher Harding recalled. "He was not seminary-trained and he did not really want a church. He liked lecturing in a theater." Elaine St. Johns stated that the building of Founders Church, in Los Angeles on 6th and New Hampshire, adjacent to the Institute of Religious Science and Philosophy, which was completed in the last months of his life, never really interested him. It was the generating force of Dr. William H. D. Hornaday that was responsible for the building of that church.

Radio talks were the only form of public speaking that Holmes found difficult. His radio program entitled *This Thing Called Life* was broadcast from 1949 to 1953. The radio studio with the prepared script and absence of a live audience did not suit his wide open style. He missed the interplay between speaker and audience which always seemed thrilling and rewarding to him. He was at heart a performer and loved a live audience.

In the mid-1950s, about five years before he died, Holmes sensed that he was not always up to par when he spoke on Sundays. He sensed that he was losing some of his power as a speaker. He told Bill Lynn, "If I'm not making sense, let me know. Don't let me destroy what I have done." Lynn, who heard him regularly, acknowledged that he was having his off days, and that he was occasionally repeating himself. In 1956, at the age of sixty nine, Holmes chose retirement from regular Sunday speaking. He told Lynn that he wanted to quit while he was still ahead.

Holmes also loved to teach, and during the many years he worked at the Institute in Los Angeles he planned and taught most of the course offerings. He was apparently as successful in the lecture hall as he was on the speaker's platform. Jack Addington, who was a student of Holmes while studying for the ministry in the 1940s, observed that his courses were the only ones in which it was impossible to take notes. "He was so compelling to listen to that you couldn't stop to take notes. By the time you stopped to take a note he was off onto something else. He was just going way ahead of you."

Holmes was intellectually curious, and it made him a good teacher. A voracious reader, he acquainted himself with every major work in the fields of metaphysics, philosophy, religion and science. He was a constant reader of sacred scripture. Though not formally educated, he overcame his limited academic background through wide reading.

Holmes was always surrounded by a stack of books. Throughout his thirty-three years as Dean of the Institute he was on the review list of several publishing houses and had standing orders in Los Angeles bookstores for all major offerings. His book and magazine bills were enormous.

Holmes was constantly exploring because he believed that his philosophy of Science of Mind should be "open at the top", as he put it, for new insights, for fresh stimulation, and revitalizing ways of teaching about matters of the spirit.

Holmes learned from people as well as books. He was always exchanging ideas and obtaining new information. Vetura Papke describes him as "the most curious individual, without being snoopy, that I ever knew. He wanted to know everything about me. what did I think about this, why did you do that?'

He also had a sharp mind. "A clear thinker" as his long-time associate Robert Bitzer remembered him, "a philosopher rather than a priest," and someone who brought a coherence and cohesiveness to the New Thought movement—something that was lacking before he arrived on the scene. Shirley McAlpine, who took several classes from him at the Institute, describes him as concise, precise and learned. He was, to her mind, an excellent interpreter; the most easily understood of all the New Thought leaders, and "a person who could pull together the teachings of others and make them understandable."

Holmes himself explained why he was constantly reading, and constantly searching. "Anything that comes along that's better than what I've got," he said, "I want to know about it." Though he was constantly learning and keeping up-to-date on spiritual teaching, his philosophy of Science of Mind, over the course of his lifetime, remained relatively stable and unchanged. While he added to and deepened his teachings, and made them more explicit, there were no major zigs or zags. Reviewing his teachings over the forty-year span of his career, Fletcher Harding, who acquainted himself in depth with Holmes' writing while serving as head of the Ministry of Education at the Institute in the 1940s, could find no major changes in his teaching, no abrupt shifts in direction.

Reginald Armor, who knew Holmes when he first came to Los Angeles before World War I, concurred with this view. "As I read the words that he wrote in the late years," said Armor, "I find that he was saying the same thing in the last days on earth as he was saying when I first met him."[3]

Many great speakers have difficulty when it comes to committing the spoken word to writing. Holmes was no exception. He was aware that the Religious Science Movement would be only as strong as the literature supporting it. From the outset of his speaking career he made a conscious effort to write. Yet writing never came easily for him. His preferred method was to have his lectures, sermons and teaching lessons transcribed in shorthand (in later years they were recorded and transcribed. He would then work with the script through a process of editing, revising and adding.

He found this to be a time-consuming and frustrating task. "The darn things never come out on paper the way they sound when I'm giving them," he complained. He tried drafting using a typewriter, but he was not a skilled typist, and the inevitable mistakes interrupted his thought processes. He expressed his frustration, saying, "It does not keep up with my ideas." He tried dictating to a secretary, but found this method to have some of the same limitations as speaking. He was still faced with the task of editing and re-writing.

Holmes had the good sense to use skilled editors to help him get his work in print when the task of writing became burdensome. Some of his most important books were written with the help of others. He received assistance from a woman in Boston who helped pull together the manuscripts that comprised his first textbook. Maude Latham, the Editor of *Science of Mind* magazine in the 1930s assisted him in preparing the revised version of the text, which was published in 1938, and reportedly drafted some of it herself.

In the latter part of his career he received assistance on several books from the then Editor of *Science of Mind* magazine, Willis Kinnear. His radio show, "This Thing Called Life," was written by Fletcher Harding when he was an employee of the Institute. Holmes was able to amass a large body of literature embodying his philosophy of Science of Mind over the course of his career because he had the good sense to enlist the support of skilled people to help him.

CHAPTER V

The Formative Years

"I was fortunate," Holmes recalled, "in being reared in a home where no religious fears were taught, and where every attempt was made to keep away from superstition and ignorance." It was a religious home, he remembered, "where family prayers were said, the Bible was read daily and grace was said at mealtime."[1]

Holmes's mother, Anna Heath Holmes, was a Congregationalist and deeply interested in religion. She saw to it that each of her eight boys, including her youngest, Ernest Shurtleff, named after a popular young preacher, attended Congregational church services and Sunday school. She gathered her brood around her for nightly readings of scripture. "I never knew anybody who took her religion more seriously," remembers his brother Fenwicke. "God was taken openly into her confidence, and we were sent to bed without doubt that He and Mother would take good care of us while we slept."

Born in 1887 in a small wooden farmhouse near Lincoln, Maine, Holmes was the product of late 19th century rural America. The family lived what his brother Fenwicke called a "semi-pioneer" existence on a small "stone-strewn, bush-threatened" Maine farm. His father, William Nelson Holmes, who traced his Scottish and English ancestry into the New England of the 17th century, was also of rural origins. He left school at the age of fourteen, and when, in his early twenties, he met his wife to be, he had just bought a hillside with a run-down house across the road from where she lived.

William Holmes was not a successful farmer. Making ends meet was always a problem. When Ernest was six the mortgage on the farm was foreclosed and the family was forced to leave. For a time they were a family on the move. "We went to live in an old rented house in the village," remembers Fenwicke, "and from there to first one and then another house that could be rented cheaply." His father worked here and there, finally getting permanent employment in a lumber camp across the state. The family followed, settling ultimately in Bethel, Maine, where Ernest was to remain until age fifteen.

The Congregationalist Church there was important. "On Sunday morning mother routed us out to Sunday school and church" recalls Fenwicke. Unlike many rural Protestant New England families, however, the Holmeses did not raise their boys in an atmosphere of religious fear. "No one talked of the Devil," recalled Fenwicke, "and no one was afraid of future punishment." Ernest agreed. "It was never suggested," he said, "that we fear God or the future."

As a boy, Holmes was intellectually curious and read a lot. His mother nicknamed him "The Question Mark" because, even at the age of five, he was always asking "Why?" In spite of his active, inquisitive mind, Holmes did not like school. Fenwicke says he found it too confining and preferred reading the Bible at home to reading history in school.

Holmes quit school at age fifteen and went to work in a wood pulp factory as a "cookie," which was a combination of a bus boy, waiter and assistant cook. "I rebelled against authority and didn't want to be taken care of," Holmes recalled, "so I went to work when I was a kid." He returned to the farm about a year later—haying crops and milking cows. Finding little challenge in farm work he, at age seventeen. went back to school, attending public high school for a few months.

Again, he found studies in English, Latin and Math not to his liking. He preferred to go to his room and read books of his own choosing. Within a short time he decided, according to Fenwicke, to leave school and "to look for learning in the world of the living." Holmes himself explained, "I didn't go to school because I didn't like it—hated it—quit when I was about fifteen. . . . What I have gathered has been from reading, studying, thinking and working. It is a long laborious tough method, but it pays off."

Holmes made an important decision in 1905 at the age of eighteen when he chose to leave rural Maine and move to the unfamiliar surroundings of metropolitan Boston. With no idea of what he would do in life or what employment he would seek, he went to live with his Aunt Carrie Steeves and her family. Up to this point in his life, Fenwicke observed, there was nothing, "physically, mentally or spiritually" either in his personality or character to suggest that he would become "an enlightened spiritual leader."

In Boston he found immediate work in the Steeve's family grocery and meat store. The family was Baptist and invited him to attend church with them. He joined the Page Bible class, but shied away from being baptized. After a period of study and further consideration he consented. "I had been brought up a Congregationalist," he later recalled, "and I saw little difference in the Baptist teaching except for the devil and whether you should be immersed or sprinkled, so I decided to take the leap."

He told his brother later that the experience did not live up to its billing. He was disappointed that the baptism did not do something to him. "I didn't feel more saved than I had before. I didn't feel different at all."

What did make a difference in his thinking about the meaning of life was, when at the age of twenty in 1907, he read the *Essays* of Ralph Waldo Emerson. He discovered them, quite by accident in the cottage of a family member. He read all day and late into the night. "When I read *Self Reliance*," he said, "it rang a bell in me. It corresponded to something I had felt, but had not thought. . . . Perhaps it was the appeal of something that I wanted to be, that I ought to be, that I was determined to be that drew me with almost dramatic intensity. . . . At that moment all I could think of was that there was more to a person than he realizes, that is beyond ordinary experience. For the first time in my life I thought that whatever was going to happen to me would be due to *something that was already in me.* . . . I believed I was on the track of an entirely new thing. I knew I would get an answer to some questions the church had not given me."

Fenwicke observed that his brother rejoiced in the feelings of freedom from the chains of ecclesiastical opinion and authority. He began to find new names for God, seeing God in ontological terms, as First Cause, Being, Impersonal Principle and Spirit. He also began focusing his attention on the philosophy of religion rather than on religion itself.

In 1908 he took a major new direction in his life when he enrolled in the Leland Powers School of Dramatic Expression in Boston. Always interested in dramatic entertainment Holmes attended a recital by Leland Powers and was astonished and entranced. Powers was a famous entertainer on the Chautauqua Circuit of New York and New England, and also conducted his own School of Expression.

After hearing Powers he decided to apply for admission to the Powers School. Powers' wife, who worked at the school, and whose rich and beautiful voice and diction had given her the position of second reader of the Mother Church of Christian Science in Boston, was impressed by the tone quality of Holmes' voice and the expressiveness in his hands. She soon took a personal interest in him and invited him to attend services at the Mother Church.

Holmes' intellectual curiosity was aroused by the message that was delivered at the service and he soon read Mary Baker Eddy's *Science and Health with Key to the Scriptures.* He was deeply impressed by it and soon could quote from it as he could from Emerson. Noting points of similarity between Eddy and Emerson he came to a conclusion that there was "a spiritual law or principle that could be called upon for healing, independent of any particular religious faith, and that anyone could use," including himself.

He had accepted from Emerson the principle that there was "something in my mind and my own being that was one with a universal consciousness." From Christian Science he began to get the main idea that was to stand at the base of his philosophy of Science of Mind. "I began to get the concept deep inside me" he noted, "that there was a Divine Presence with whom I could commune, but there was also a Divine Law which I could use."

The most important result of his study of Emerson and Mrs. Eddy, he said, was that he now knew that "God is good." Until this time he viewed God as passive, not active. "Now I believed He was working at it and you could go along with Him."

While Christian Science was important to Holmes he never joined the church. He believed in its major principles, deeply respected Mrs. Eddy and her movement, always defended her against criticism, but never himself became a Christian Scientist. He found himself more attracted, as time went on, to other writers associated with the New Thought movement.

"I was a natural candidate for the New Thought philosophies that have sprung up in this country," he remembered. "Having read Emerson it was easy to realize that Unity is the basis of everything." He soon was exploring the writings of Christian D. Larson, Ralph Waldo Trine, Horatio Dresser and Phineas Quimby. Holmes was particularly impressed with the New Thought writings of Larson. According to Fenwicke he abandoned the Christian Science textbook for Larson's works.

It was in Boston that Holmes first experimented with Spiritual Mind Treatment. One of the first persons he "worked for" (Holmes told almost everyone he "treated" that he would "work" for them) was a fellow classmate at the Powers School. Though a student of public speaking the young man was suffering from stage fright. The treatment was apparently effective as the man's timidity on the platform, according to Holmes, never recurred. In later reflection on the success of that treatment, Holmes observed that all he had really done was to get the young man to "think the same thing I was thinking. He was reflecting my mind."

Members of the Steeves family, who were at first dubious and skeptical, wondering how he could give treatment without taking Christian Science class work, soon asked him to treat for them. The treatment was apparently successful as one of the members of the Steeves family reportedly told him, "I don't know what you do, but please do it." The growing number of "demonstrations" proved to him that he was doing something right because he was getting results. He was encouraged. "So I kept on," he recalled.

It was at this time that Holmes treated for his mother who was suffering from heart trouble. According to Fenwicke he "worked up a complete argument." Ernest remembers, "I half asked God to heal her and half affirmed that He would." Again, the treatment apparently worked as his mother, without other medical intervention, got over the heart trouble and was never again bothered by it, dying of other causes at the age of 98. He concluded that in his mother's case, "I changed my consciousness about her and it in some way reached her. I didn't know how it happened, but it did."

In later years, Fenwicke, in questioning Ernest on the development of his philosophical system, pressed him on the question of whether by 1909 at age 22 he had "a full blown philosophy" and a workable method of Spiritual Mind Treatment. Ernest replied, "It was in the egg, an embryo, half-hatched, but pipping at the shell." Fenwicke believed that it was not until four or five years later that his brother formulated a systematic method of treatment. Ernest would probably have agreed with that view.

While in Boston, Holmes also explored spiritual mediumship (a form of psychic functioning), which was gaining popularity in the early 1900s in New England. Holmes learned about a man named Wiggin who held spiritualist meetings on Sunday nights in Jordan Hall of the Conservatory of Music. He began to regularly attend Wiggin's seances. Holmes recalls that he was "terrifically impressed." Yet he was never totally convinced of the value, importance and reliability of the information that came through the medium. "They just go so far," he remembered, "and never any further."

CHAPTER VI

Working With Fenwicke

Holmes left Boston for Califor-
nia in 1912 after finishing his studies at the Powers School. The
move to California was occasioned by an invitation from his
brother, Fenwicke, to visit him and his mother in Venice, California,
a seacoast town about 15 miles west of Los Angeles, where Fenwicke
was now pastor of a Congregationalist church.

Fenwicke describes Ernest on his arrival as "exuberant, ro-
bust, not tall, but extremely dynamic," and prepared for a career as
a platform entertainer. Instead of returning to the East after his visit,
Ernest decided to stay in California and live with Fenwicke until he
got established. Soon he had name cards printed advertising himself as an entertainer.[1]

Immediate work was not forthcoming, so, in addition to
helping his brother with the junior church, the young men's club
and the boy scout troop, he secured a position as playground
director for the grammar school. In his free time he continued with
his study of metaphysics. He discovered a metaphysical library in
the Brach Shops, an office building on 7th Street in downtown Los
Angeles, and became a regular visitor and borrower of books.

It was here that he came across *The Edinburgh Lectures in
Mental Science* and a companion book, *The Dore Lectures* by Judge
Thomas Troward. Fenwicke observed that finding Troward "filled

him with overwhelming delight." Troward's theoretical work on the practice of mental healing opened new vistas for him. "It eclipsed anything I ever read," Holmes commented. "In fact, I couldn't help saying to myself, 'this is exactly what I feel. This solves the problem of dualities. This is the real meaning of Principle. This is the Law.'"

After getting settled in Venice, Holmes continued the practice begun in Boston of giving treatment. Fenwicke reports a healing of a woman by the name of Mrs. Brown who showed up at the parsonage one day demanding to see Ernest and "get treatment." A victim of recurring abdominal pains, she often felt that she was on the point of death. She stayed two weeks, during which time Ernest treated. When she left, Ernest said, "she was perfectly well." Holmes kept in touch with the woman, and became "firm friends," and was pleased that the sickness never recurred.

An unexpected catalyst to Holmes's spiritual work came in 1914 from an unlikely source. He was offered a job by H. B. Eakin, a friend he met at Fenwicke's church, as purchasing agent for the city of Venice. The job required his physical presence in the city purchasing department, but gave him maximum free time on the job. Afforded a private office he was able to continue his reading and studying while at work. He could also do occasional healing work in his office.

Eakin noticed the books on philosophy, metaphysics and the occult that Holmes had lying around the office and borrowed some of them. Eakin, discussing some of the books with Holmes, became fascinated by Holmes's knowledge and learning, and said to him, "How would you like to come over to my house and I will invite a few people one evening and you can just talk to us." Holmes accepted and used the opportunity to discuss before a gathering of about twenty people the *Edinburgh Lectures of Troward* and some of his own ideas on mental healing.

Shortly after he began speaking at evenings in the Eakin home he was invited to be one of the speakers for regular noon-day lectures held at the Metaphysical library in downtown Los Angeles. The Director, Mrs. Reeseberg, had learned of his work from two women whom he had successfully treated. In addition to giving a lecture, Holmes was asked to teach a class afterward explaining the philosophy and theory of treatment of Troward.

Holmes agreed, and to his surprise thirteen people stayed over from the lecture and attended his class, paying twenty five cents each. After the class he announced that he would give treatment to anyone who wanted his help. Fenwicke recalls that everyone was pleased with his work, and Mrs. Reeseberg most of all. She asked him to become a regular speaker at the library. Fenwicke credits the speech at the Metaphysical library as marking the beginning of his career as a "public exponent of practical and applied metaphysics."

Shortly thereafter in 1916, Ernest convinced Fenwicke to help him write and edit a magazine on mental healing. Fenwicke, who had become increasingly interested in metaphysics, agreed, even though the material to be published would not be usable in his ministry at the Congregational church. Ernest contributed an article each month and formulated some treatments. The magazine, entitled *Uplift*, immediately began to draw people to Ernest as a practitioner and increased his visibility in the community.

Soon he received offers to lecture one day each week at the Vista del Arroyo Hotel in Pasadena and the Schuyler Hotel in Long Beach. Requests for treatment increased to the point that he needed to find space other than his office at the purchasing department to do the work. He rented a summer cottage in Venice from Annie Gillan, who was to become his future mother-in-law. Here he was able to do treatment at night and to offer private classes on weekends. Finally in 1916 he was generating sufficient income so that he could give up his job with the city for full time teaching and healing.

As his following increased, he decided to seek ordination as a minister of Divine Science. The Church of Divine Science, like Unity School of Christianity, was a New Thought church, and its teachings were in consonance with his beliefs. As a Divine Science minister his healing treatments would have the sanction of the church. In addition he could perform marriages, which he was now being asked to do. On the recommendation of a Mrs. Graham, a woman who had come to work with him at the healing center in Venice, he went to Seattle to meet with Mrs. Agnes T. Galer, a minister of Divine Science there.

Mrs. Galer, who was conducting a successful ministry, was authorized by the Divine Science Church to confer ordination. After spending time with Holmes, she became convinced that Holmes had sufficient metaphysical knowledge and ability to serve as a minister and ordained him.

In 1917 Fenwicke decided to give up his Congregational ministry and join Ernest in his metaphysical work. Fenwicke no longer believed in the Christian message as taught by the Congregational Church and felt it was time to move on to other things. Ernest had urged him to make a change. "You don't believe it anymore," Ernest told Fenwicke. "Why try to preach it?"

Fenwicke was uneasy because he wasn't sure he could make it financially. Ernest encouraged him so he decided to take the plunge. "I suppose that in my heart I knew I would go on with Ernest," Fenwicke recalled, "for it took little persuasion from him to join in expanding the work. I was half in it anyway because of *Uplift.*

The brothers decided to open their own lecture hall in the Brach shops, feeling they had outgrown the capacity of the Metaphysical Library, and to speak on Sundays at the Strand theater. In addition, they decided to give up their cottage in Venice for a big residence in Long Beach that could be opened up as a sanitarium for those who sought metaphysical help. Money for the purchase was obtained in part from the sale of Fenwicke's home in Venice. The Long Beach facility was a big three-story Victorian house with a round tower. Rooms were built in the garage so that the sanitarium could accommodate eighteen patients.

The brothers organized their work at the new facility in Long Beach, in the Brach shops in Los Angeles, and at the Strand theater under the name of the Southern California New Thought Institute. Fenwicke reported that within ten days every room at the Long Beach sanitarium was full. Those who came, according to Fenwicke, were people suffering from "psychoneurosis and associated disorders."

Evidently, many of the patients were women. They were afflicted, he said, with "ennui." The meaning of life had been lost, "perhaps because their children had grown up and gone out into the world, leaving them little or nothing to do." Other patients included soldiers returning from World War I who were suffering from shell shock. Fenwicke observed that Ernest was particularly adept at dealing with "psychoneurotic cases" of men returning from battle. When patients were not being given Spiritual Mind Treatment they were engaged, according to Fenwicke, in some kind of creative work, "knitting, painting and other forms of artistic self-expression."

It was shortly after the brothers began working together that Ernest recognized the importance of putting his philosophical ideas and knowledge of treatment in writing into book form. After a lecture or class, students wanted something to take home to read. *Uplift* magazine was a help, but a book would be more substantial. He began work in 1917 on *Creative Mind* and shortly thereafter on *Creative Mind and Success* and within two years both were published. Fenwicke believed that in these two books his brother presented a well developed philosophy of mind, and that the books incorporated "the whole philosophy and practice of Science of Mind." While Fenwicke acknowledged that Ernest would later enrich and supplement it with new knowledge in the fields of science, philosophy, mysticism and psychology, his basic ideas would not be greatly modified.

On the speaking platform Ernest was coming into his own. On Sundays at the Strand theater he was speaking to a sizable audience. Fenwicke noted with admiration that Ernest "spoke like a man of authority, and as one inspired." Recognizing his own limitations Fenwicke acknowledged that "in spite of my formal education and platform experience, I couldn't hold a candle to him. I was too much the minister and too little the metaphysician."

The brothers divided up the work so that Fenwicke spent most of his time at the sanitarium in Long Beach while Ernest lectured and gave treatment at the Brach shops in Los Angeles. Ernest was now speaking several times a week around the city, and holding meetings on Tuesday and Thursday afternoons in the Brach shops. Fenwicke felt they had made significant headway. He observed that they were doing "by far the most extensive and successful work in metaphysics in the Los Angeles area, and perhaps the country, with the exception of Christian Science, Divine Science and Unity."

Then in 1918 Fenwicke decided that he no longer wanted to operate the sanitarium in Long Beach. He concluded that his greatest interest was in platform work, and that he did not enjoy being a sanitarium superintendent and a magazine publisher. Fenwicke, unlike Ernest, had an excellent formal education, graduating Phi Beta Kappa from Colby College and receiving his ministerial training at Hartford Theological Seminary.

The brothers closed the sanitarium, sold the property and moved the family into a residence near the Brach shops. They also shut down *Uplift* magazine, concluding that it had already served its purposes. Fenwicke then joined Ernest in the teaching and healing work in the Brach Shops. The lecture halls were always crowded, said Fenwicke, and the income from classes, lectures and healing treatments met their needs.

In 1918 Fenwicke decided to accept an invitation to speak at a conference of New Thought leaders in Boston. Instead of returning to Los Angeles he went to New York City and obtained work as a lecturer for a New Thought organization called "The League for the Larger Life." He spoke several times each day and reported that there were large crowds at each meeting. In early 1919 he returned to Los Angeles elated with his success. He urged Ernest to shut down the work in Los Angeles and return with him to New York.

It is not clear why Ernest decided to leave Los Angeles where his work was prospering to lecture and teach on the East Coast. Fenwicke says it was because Ernest liked working as a team and wanted to accommodate his (Fenwicke's) desire to follow up on his success in New York. Undoubtedly, Ernest felt that if things did not work out in the East he could return to Los Angeles and pick up where he left off. In any event, in 1919 the brothers, with their mother, left for New York and launched upon what Fenwicke called "the unknown seas of itinerant lectureship."

Their work in New York City was apparently successful. They found rooms in the Schuyler Hotel in Manhattan, got help from the League for the Larger Life, and put small ads in the newspaper. "From the first," Fenwicke recalled with delight, "the crowds descended on us in a deluge. We were astonished at the numbers who came to our hotel for metaphysical advice and treatment."

Their success in New York City was followed by well attended lectures in Boston and Philadelphia. All we had to do, said Fenwicke was to place a couple of one-inch ads in the newspaper and the theaters would be crowded on Sundays. "I can only account for it," Fenwicke said, "on the grounds that the time was ripe."

It is not clear why about 18 months later, in 1920, the brothers discontinued their work in the East, returned to Los Angeles, and resumed full time teaching and healing work. Deciding that the lecture hall in the Brach shops were too small, they rented a hall in the Trinity Auditorium and built private consultation rooms on the side. They stayed three years, but never recaptured the following they enjoyed before leaving. They were unable to attract old students or interest new ones in sufficient numbers to make the work economically viable.

Fenwicke had no good explanation for their failure and decided in 1922 to return to the East. "I was not willing," he said, "to wait for another success and decided to return to the itinerant lecture field." Shortly thereafter, Ernest followed. He abandoned Los Angeles for the East Coast when he heard that things were going well for Fenwicke there. They took an apartment together there, and Ernest, rather than engaging in regular lecturing and teaching, spent the bulk of his time writing. He was working on the book that would become the first Science of Mind textbook.

Fenwicke reported that when the brothers lectured in New York and Philadelphia they again attracted large crowds. It was during the time they were in New York (1924) that Ernest sought out and studied with the highly respected metaphysical teacher Emma Curtis Hopkins. The value of her teaching, Ernest felt, resulted from the fact that "she not only experienced the consciousness of the mystic herself, but imparted spiritual connection in such a way as to awaken a corresponding consciousness in her students."

For the rest of his life he credited Hopkins with introducing him to the "limitless possibilities of practical mysticism." She was the only one he ever knew about, he said, "who combined mysticism with the use of the metaphysical principle of healing."

In 1925 the brothers discontinued working together. Fenwicke gives no explanation, other than Ernest decided to return to Los Angeles and Fenwicke wanted to continue working in the East. Reginald Armor said there were differences of opinion that caused them to go their separate ways. Bill Lynn surmised that Ernest did not like the fact that his brother was a "leaner" who took more than he gave. He wanted to have the experience of working separately.

Elaine St. Johns saw their separation as a "natural unfoldment. No big deal." Ernest wanted to teach and the most fertile field he found was the West Coast. Fenwicke wanted to preach and he had gained a strong foothold in the East.[2]

Fenwicke took over as minister of the Church of the Healing Christ in New York City (a large well-established New Thought church), while Ernest, according to Reginald Armor, "wanted larger groups on his own, not something he shared with his older brother. He sensed larger goals. He was ready for greater experiences. He wanted to teach."

CHAPTER VII

We Are A Teaching And Healing Order

When Holmes returned to Los Angeles in 1925 it had been six years since he had worked successfully there. He was for practical purposes starting over, with no assurance of success. He still felt, according to Reginald Armor, "a tremendous mission to demonstrate what he believed."[1]

He began by leasing the Ambassador Theater and speaking on Sundays. The crowds were small at first, only 75 people when he started. In a few months, however, the theater was crowded to its capacity of 625. Two years later in 1927 the Sunday morning talks were moved to the Ebell Theater which seated 1,295. Within a year that auditorium was too small, and the Sunday morning service in 1929 was moved to the Sola de Ora room of the Biltmore Hotel in the heart of downtown Los Angeles. Holmes spoke there for five years when again the crowds became greater than the seating capacity and his Sunday talks were moved to the larger Wiltern Theater at Wilshire and Western Avenues where 2,800 people could be accommodated.

Reginald Armor reports that "here again the successful performance of the previous years was repeated, and it wasn't long before we were turning away 400 to 500 people on Sunday. There was just no place to put the crowd that came to hear Ernest during those years." Armor was awed by the rapid growth of the crowds, seeing it as "nothing short of phenomenal." Everywhere Holmes spoke "the people came from far and near. Even the stage and back stage were crowded at his lectures."

With the large turn-outs on Sundays it was possible to set up weekly classes to teach courses on Science of Mind. At first people could enroll for a series of lessons for a fee of $25.00. Soon Holmes established a fifty two week long study program which came to be known as "the Major Course" in Religious Science.

In 1925 after he first began his early classes were sparsely attended, yet by the early 1930s over 100 people were graduated annually from the year-long course. In the early years Holmes himself did most of the teaching. As attendance grew the teaching staff was expanded. Holmes was pleased that by 1930 there existed a corps of teachers who were, as he noted, "extremely capable of assisting and giving the course."

Courses were soon being offered both in the daytime and in the evening, and upon completion of the one year program students received a certificate which recognized them as a "major student of Religious Science." Since spiritual mind treatment was the principal component of the course, many students, upon completion, called themselves practitioners of Religious Science.

As Holmes himself had done a decade earlier, they began devoting all or part of their time to the mental healing of others. At the outset Holmes did not require formal credentialing. It was possible for anyone who graduated from the major course to work professionally as a practitioner of spiritual mind treatment.

Holmes was convinced that if his teaching was to succeed he needed literature to support it. Any group, he commented, "needs an increasing literary outlet to go with it." When he resumed teaching in Los Angeles in 1925 he had two small books on creative thought written before he had left for the East seven years before, but he did not have a textbook he could use for teaching.

The text he had begun working on while in the East in 1920 was now nearing completion. A Boston school teacher, Ann Shipman, was helping him, and in two years the book was completed. Entitled *Science of Mind*, and published in 1927, the book gave him, he said, "a teaching textbook at last." He used it in all the courses he taught. Revised and updated in 1938 it remained throughout his lifetime and continues today as a basic tool for teaching his philosophy.

Holmes also believed that it was necessary, for sustaining and building an interest in Religious Science, to publish a monthly magazine. In 1927 he created *Religious Science* magazine (its name was changed two years later to *Science of Mind*) for the purpose of presenting to readers "a systematic and comprehensive study of the subtle powers of mind and spirit. . . . and to show how such powers may be consciously used for the betterment of the individual and the race." Holmes considered the publication to be a "semi-religious periodical. . . . ethical in its tendency, moral in its tone, which will seek to promote that universal consciousness of life which binds all together in one great whole."

He considered the magazine, according to William H. D. Hornaday, to be one of Religious Science's "greatest outreach instruments". He wanted the magazine to include affirmations, a meditation for each day of the month, inspirational stories and substantive articles teaching Science of Mind. For thirty years Holmes himself contributed an article for almost every issue. While many were transcriptions of sermons, the articles gave him an opportunity to express what was of current importance to him and to deepen the content of his philosophy. An enduring feature of the magazine has been a listing of Religious Science practitioners, ministers and churches.

As more and more people became involved with his teaching, graduates of his courses began urging Holmes to establish a formal organization to guide the growing Religious Science Movement. When he was first approached by a group of prominent Los Angeles businessmen who had attended his courses, he resisted. In his mind at that time the idea of organization meant "church," and according to Reginald Armor, "he would have none of it." He had been very emphatic about it. As Armor states, "Ernest would have no church, and he himself would not permit any competition with established churches, of which he always felt there were too many."

Unable to get anywhere with Holmes, these businessmen, who were graduates of his courses, went to Reginald Armor. "There were long sessions far into the night," recalled Armor. The argument advanced for organizing was one Holmes himself had used: "We shouldn't be selfish and keep this (teaching) just for ourselves. It needs to be given to the world." Holmes finally acquiesced, though he was extremely reluctant to become a part of a formal structure. At the outset he wanted no position on the Board of Governors of the proposed new Institute of Religious Science and Philosophy. Though he later reconsidered, when the Institute was first organized Holmes said, "My job is to deliver the water of life and keep it flowing." The task of the Board was to "post signs showing people where to find it."

The original Board of the Institute, which was formally incorporated in 1927, consisted of, in addition to Holmes, O. H. Clinch, a prominent real estate dealer, Harrison Lewis, a real estate broker, Frank B. Hathaway, a retired superintendent of the Hathaway School for Underprivileged Children, Robert Hendry, a businessman in oil well supply, J. Farrell McDonald, a character actor in the silent movies, Armor himself, and Lem Brumson, affectionately called "The Deacon," who was a developer of the Santa Fe Springs Oil District and later the famous Bel Air District. Brumson, who was one of the Board's wealthiest members, became its first chairman, and it was his personal funding that made possible the publication of *Science of Mind* magazine.

Armor recalls that there was one thing that the entire Board had in common. "We were all rebels as far as orthodox religion was concerned." Holmes went out of his way to insist that the Institute was not a religious organization or church. "The Institute," he emphasized, "is not a church, subscribes to no creed, observes no particular custom, ritual or performance."

While Holmes disavowed any religious connection, the Sunday "conferences" as he called them, held under the auspices of the Institute, had many of the characteristics of a church service. Reginald Armor observed, from a 1932 copy of a Sunday bulletin of a service conducted by Holmes at the Biltmore, that it was indeed a "church-type service", even to the extent "of an opening hymn, and having that old established post-meditation hymn so familiar to Religious Science churches everywhere, 'Open My Eyes.'" As usual the program showed that there was good professional music, Armor noted, "including a prelude by a pianist on this particular day and a violin solo during the Offertory."

It was not long after the Institute was organized that the Board of Trustees began to recognize the religious character of its activities. An advisory committee to the Board stated in a 1929 report that "a fact that was brought out in unmistakable terms was that regardless of its name or ultimate purpose, the Institute of Religious Science is essentially a religious institution, a place where people go to find satisfaction for that soul hunger which is inherent in all normal people, that it is and by its nature must continue to be a substitute for the church, which they, for the most part, left to become associated with it."

The committee then unanimously recommended that the religious aspects of the Institute be regarded as paramount, and its educational activities be considered as incidental to its primary mission. Holmes, who attended the Board meeting at which this report was presented, offered no objections.[2]

Yet Holmes himself, for several years after the Institute was founded, clung to the notion that he was espousing a spiritual teaching, and not building a new institutional church. He encouraged ministers from other religions to come to the Institute, not to become Religious Scientists, but to learn the principles of Science of Mind, and according to Armor, "take the teaching and philosophy back to their own churches."

Headquarters for the new Institute was established on the second floor of an office building at 2511 Wilshire Boulevard. In addition to a business office and practitioners quarters there was a library, a lecture hall and a publications room which was occupied by *Science of Mind* magazine. Within a short time the Institute was a very active place.

A check of its weekly events indicates that the days between the Sunday services were filled with church-related activities. A

Men's Forum and a Women's Forum met on Monday evenings. There was a Bible interpretation on Tuesday and a meditation service and instruction on Wednesday evenings. On Thursdays there was a Mother's Roundtable, and on Fridays at 2:00 P.M. there were self-help talks for the purpose of aiding individuals to apply the principles of Religious Science in daily life, and on Friday evenings there were the Troward lectures given by Holmes himself.

The major course in Religious Science was taught three days each week in the mornings and in the evenings. On Sunday mornings Institute headquarters was host at 11:00 A.M. to Sunday School and Junior Institute.

By 1930 important steps had been taken to make Religious Science a viable spiritual movement. As Reginald Armor observed, Holmes had "his textbook. He had his teaching institute. He had his magazine." In addition, on Sundays he was often speaking to congregations of over 3,000 people. The decade of the 1930s was to be even more fruitful.

As the number of practitioners grew the Board of the Institute decided to sponsor a "Healing Department." A fore-runner of the current Ministry of Prayer at the United Church of Religious Science in Los Angeles, the Healing Department was comprised of practitioners who treated for those who requested help by mail or telephone call. The ministry was maintained in particular for those who were unable to procure the services of a professional practitioner. The group met daily at 11:00 A.M. in the Institute's meditation room and conducted healing meditation.

A program to make practitioners more professional was initiated in the early 1930s. This effort was in part in response to reports that several practitioners were introducing techniques in their work which were contrary to the teaching and practice of Religious Science. "Imagine," wrote Reginald Armor, "practitioners prognosticating on the basis of reading bumps on the head or from handwriting specimens." Armor also reported that it was learned that a practitioner in San Francisco was asking clients for their exact date and time of birth so that a horoscope could be cast.

The practitioner purportedly told the client, "In this way we will know how to work more intelligently in this situation for you."

In an effort to prevent abuses in the Institute in 1932 authorized a credentialing system for practitioners which required those who wished to practice professionally to take a specified curriculum of courses and to demonstrate their ability to treat by documenting their successes with clients. While the details of the "Practitioner Professional Training Course" were not fully implemented until later in the decade, the new system ultimately gave practitioners a stronger professional footing.

As the work of the Institute became more and more successful, Holmes began looking for ways to expand the work. By 1930 he began to see the Institute not just as a training ground for practitioners and for people who wanted to learn the principles of Science of Mind, but as a school of philosophical training. Persons might learn the principles and then go to other cities and start centers which would follow the Institute model.

Holmes began looking for people who had the ability to carry on this work. As Reginald Armor observed, "there was a constant stream of personalities through the door of the Institute in his seeking for key people to assist in the growth." Many of them were ministers from other churches or professionals in the field of education.

As a part of this effort in 1930 he encouraged Robert Bitzer, a young minister of mental science, who he had met and worked with in Boston several years before, to come to Los Angeles and organize a branch of the Institute in Hollywood. While the Institute provided no funds, Holmes himself assisted Bitzer in building the congregation. Holmes, explained that he helped Bitzer by speaking for him at the Women's Club in Hollywood on a Sunday afternoon. "We wanted everybody to come," said Holmes, "and we had about 800 people. I told them we were going to start a chapter there and Dr. Bitzer was to be the head of it. That's the way the church got started."

As the 1930s progressed other branches were started. "They were surpluses," Holmes said, from the Wiltern services which he conducted. After helping Bitzer in Hollywood, Holmes did the same thing for other leaders in Huntington Park, Santa Monica and Redondo Beach and other places. Again, no seed money was provided by the Institute. A leader was selected by the Institute and Holmes would, according to Armor, establish a "focalizing interest in the new locality by giving talks there." From then on leaders relied on their own resources.

As Robert Bitzer commented, "I never received any financial help. Dr. Holmes did not believe in financing a new minister. He felt that the minister must do it on his own. If he had it, he would make it."[3]

By the end of the 1930s the Institute was holding Sunday services at five sites in the Los Angeles area. Holmes's anti-church attitude was still manifest in his plans for these new extensions of the Institute. He would not allow the branches to call themselves churches nor would he allow their leaders to call themselves ministers.

In 1939 an important development occurred in the growth of the Religious Science movement. The Board of Trustees authorized the branches of the Institute to incorporate as separate chapters. This allowed these groups, not only to conduct Sunday services and teach courses, but to own property and elect their own boards of directors. Leaders, if they had credentials, were also allowed to call themselves ministers if they so desired.

By-laws and an organization plan were adopted for the chapters and general rules set forth. The activities of the chapter were confined to the teaching and practice of Religious Science and to the cultural and social welfare of its individual members. The responsibilities of active members of the chapter were also spelled out. A primary responsibility was "to uphold the teachings and practice of Religious Science by continuous effort to grow therein and to exemplify them in daily life." The manner of engagement and tenure of the "speaker or minister" was also described.

Status as a chapter of the Institute was granted if a Religious Science group in a locality could demonstrate that it had fifty active members. The group was required to formally apply to the Institute for chapter status, and that application had to be formally approved by the Board of Trustees.

The formation of chapters coincided with a decision by the Board of Trustees to ordain ministers. In the fall of 1938 the attorney for the Institute was instructed to determine whether the organization had legal authority to confer ordination. When he determined that the Institute in fact had the legal power, the Board established policies governing ordination. It was stipulated that only such persons who had met the educational requirements of the Institute and were needed as ministers and assistant ministers shall be ordained. Holmes, who had been originally ordained as a Divine Science minister now underwent official ordination as a minister of the "Gospel of Religious Science."

The ordination of ministers, in addition to the official establishment of chapters, further strengthened the view among people involved with Religious Science that they were in fact—if not in name—a church. "It was only logical," says Reginald Armor, "that many people began to think and speak of their chapters as churches of Religious Science. They would say, 'We are for all intents and purposes conducting the activities of a church, so we are going to call our chapters a church.'" Nevertheless, the word "church" had not been included in the chapter by-laws, and its use in describing Religious Science activities had not been sanctioned by the Institute's Board.

Holmes, who still referred to his Sunday morning meetings at the Wiltern as "conferences" was not pleased when he learned that chapter members were referring to themselves as churches. He never acted, however, to stop it, and within a short time several chapters requested that the Institute recognize them officially as churches of Religious Science. "It wasn't planned that way," Reginald Armor later observed, "but the Institute moved away from the purely esoteric school idea, and the idea of church began to take hold."

In the early 1940s Holmes finally accepted the idea of ministers and churches. He did this, Vetura Papke believed, because he wanted his work to remain popular after he passed from the scene.

He had come to the conclusion that the philosophy of Religious Science must be perpetuated, and that the only way that would happen was through churches.

In later years Holmes finally decided, according to Craig Carter, that Religious Science would not make you a better something else. "We used to say," Holmes was to recall, "that Religious Science would make a better Methodist of a Methodist, a better Presbyterian of a Presbyterian, but I have come to the conclusion that if you really understand Religious Science you could not continue being a Presbyterian or a Methodist." It took some time, said Carter, but Holmes by the 1950s finally came to realize that "we are ourselves, we are a sect, we are a denomination."

A reflection of Holmes's changed attitude can be seen in his advice to practitioners who were graduating from the Institute. "Now go out and heal," he told them at graduation exercises. "Do the thing. Be the thing itself. Don't worry about being a success. Wherever you have an audience, if there is one person healed of a problem, people will flock to your doorstep. So great is the need. This is the way the church will grow."

Holmes had finally come to the conclusion, according to Reginald Armor, that the growth of the movement was vitally important. "He wanted a world wide organization. . . . and he was seeking to multiply himself." Holmes recognized that the Movement flourished when leaders were developed who, like himself, had highly developed skills as dynamic speakers. The ability to speak inspirationally was the key. Congregations demanded it. Holmes knew that he himself could, by speaking in a new locality, build an audience for a new leader. But the critical question that always arose was, "Can the new leader keep it?"

Unfortunate as it might be, he lamented, "You cannot educate people away from preaching." If a minister was not a good speaker the church floundered. "You can teach a ministerial candidate all there is to know about metaphysics and comparative religions," he said, "but until he gets up in front of an audience, you'll never know." Leadership from the pulpit was vitally essential. "We grew as fast," he said, "as we could develop good leaders."

As the movement grew Holmes became increasingly concerned with maintaining the integrity of the teaching. He wanted to be sure that the Institute continued to be its originating source, controlling the dissemination of all Religious Science literature. In 1943 in a letter to an associate in he expressed his concern regarding deviations which cropped up as new branches and new ministers came into the movement. "When we found it necessary to have branches," he stated, "we found it equally necessary to organize the work with enough authority to make it impossible for the branches to institute a teaching entirely separate and different from ours."

Heresy was apparently a continuing problem. The Board approved a policy that in order to maintain the integrity of the teaching that "only the teaching of Religious Science be permitted by our Institute speakers." The Board also approved a policy, at the suggestion of Holmes, that no lecture series by outside speakers could be given unless authorized by the Board.

Literature published by anyone, anywhere, under the name of Religious Science was also subjected to scrutiny. In 1947 the Board approved a policy which required that all materials be submitted to a committee of the Board for approval. The policy stated, "Any book, treatise, or pamphlet written to be published by anyone, which publication is purported to be under the auspices or, recommended by the Institute, or if the name of the Institute is to appear on the publication, such manuscript is to be submitted to the Literature Committee of the Institute for approval."

The action of the Board and Holmes in exercising tight control over the teachings of Religious Science seems to contradict a position that Holmes held in regard to all his teaching— that is that it was "open at the top for new understandings and insights." Holmes often stressed that Religious Science "should revere all religious concepts," and that the Science of Mind was "never a closed book" but continued to gather spiritual truths "from every source and every person's experience."

It seems that Holmes was of two minds on additions to the teaching. He believed that he had developed a system of thought "which keeps faith with the best conclusions of the ages," and did not want others, particularly his own ministers, diluting or distorting it. At the same time he did not want to leave the impression that he considered his teaching a final revelation which must at all costs be maintained in its purity as the authoritative basis of Religious Science.

Vetura Papke believed that Holmes would have disapproved of many things that have been added to the teaching since his death. While Holmes was not inflexible regarding updating or changing his teaching, she said, "he did not mean that it should be considered totally 'open at the top'."

During the 1930s the Institute constantly struggled to keep itself financially solvent. While little financial information is available (this writer could find no annual reports of income and expenses prior to 1954) the minutes of meetings of the Board of Trustees constantly allude to problems of over-spending deficits. The budget for 1930 had a projected $15,000 deficit, and part of that was financed by a $3,000 loan from Holmes. The money was used for paying past due current bills. In 1932 it was estimated that it would cost about $64,000 to operate, and with a projected income from classes, publications and Sunday collections at the Wiltern totaling about $30,000, a deficit of $34,000 was anticipated. It was indicated that a special contribution would be needed to keep the Institute afloat.

The financial difficulties that the Institute experienced in the 1930s did not prevent it in 1935 from purchasing at a cost of $47,000 a beautiful large building on the corner of 6th and New Hampshire in Los Angeles to serve as Institute headquarters. Built originally as an office for interior decorators it had ample space for classrooms, practitioner and business offices, a lecture hall, meditation room and library.

The building, however, was not suitable for church services, especially for the large groups that Holmes was attracting. It is indicative of the strength of Holmes's initial vision— that he wanted an educational institution rather than a denominational church— that he decided to put the Institute's resources into space that could be used for teaching and practice rather than for church services.

Holmes himself drew a salary from the Institute. The amount totaled $10,000 annually. Throughout his years at the Institute that sum never changed. He was paid $10,000 during his first year at the Institute and $10,000 in his last year.

In the early years Holmes, as Dean of the Institute, was chief operating officer, responsible for managing the educational program, practitioner work, and the publication effort as well as the hiring, firing and finances. The President of the Institute, Lem Brumson, was not involved in the day-to-day operation.

Brumson was the first of a series of Presidents who held office during Holmes' thirty-year tenure as Dean of the Institute. As chief executive officer, the Institute's president was the legally responsible corporate officer and was technically Holmes' superior in the organization. Although Holmes was never president of the organization or a corporate officer he maintained *de facto* management control over the Institute and its affairs through a power of permanent trusteeship accorded to him in the by-laws.

This power, accorded to Holmes and Holmes alone, gave him the right to ask for and receive the resignation of any member of the Board of Trustees at any time, including the corporate officers. Holmes' continuing control of the management of the Institute was further assured because the Board itself was organized as a self-perpetuating group, not subject to re-election from a voting membership. The Board could re-elect itself at the end of proscribed terms, or act to fill a vacancy through retirement or resignation. Holmes played a central role in the selection process serving almost always on the Board's nominating committee. Holmes, as permanent trustee, had a life tenure and was not himself subject to election.

Though Holmes had a distaste for administrative detail he was, until 1938 when a general manager was appointed, deeply involved in the nitty gritty. A case in point involves salary raises for employees of the Institute. Holmes reported to the Board on March 15, 1934 that he felt that Mrs. Helen Carmack's salary "should be increased fifteen dollars a month to be paid by the magazine, making her salary $125 per month". He also stated that he felt "that in some way Mrs. Myrtle Keith should receive a certain percentage of the gross receipts from the tuition paid to classes." These are just two examples of many problems of an administrative nature that Holmes, in his role as Dean, involved himself.

The financial troubles that periodically troubled the Institute in the 1930s continued into the 1940s. Operating capital was so tight in 1941 that money had to be borrowed to finance correspondence courses. Holmes himself continued to lend money to the Institute. By 1941 several thousand dollars was owed him. In order to get the Institute back on a more even footing Holmes loaned $12,000 in 1941. William Haughey, who had taken over as President in 1938, and who also assumed the role of general manager, reported in 1943 and 1945 that the financial status of the organization was gradually improving, but in 1947 funds again were so tight that several employees were asked to take leaves of absence during the summer.

By the end of the decade the Institute had still not paid its debt to Holmes. Then in February 1951, Holmes again lent $10,000. This apparently was not enough as in December 1951, Larry Atwood, the new President recommended that Board reductions in personnel and salary rates were needed so that expenses could be brought within income.

It was not until 1954 that the Institute became financially solvent. Bill Lynn, who was on the staff of the Institute from 1953 to 1989, and who was deeply involved in its financial affairs, explains what happened.

When the staff discovered that under the IRS code a church could own a business, the church began entering into business deals. Businesses were bought with no down payment, with the idea that the mortgages would be paid off out of earnings. Lawyers, brokers, promoters— often church members— brought these deals to the church. It seemed like an appropriate thing to do since other churches, including the Catholics and Mormons were doing it. Most of the transactions were not profitable.

The church benefited from the fact that two of these businesses became very successful. One that was particularly lucrative involved patents for sink frames which had been developed by a group of plumbers in Chicago whose business was called "Hudy Sink". This was the 1950s and it was the era of formica countertops in kitchens and baths. Hudy Sink had developed a rim called the "Hudy Rim", and had a patent in 1954 that had several years to run. The church bought the patents at a favorable price and then entered into a licensing agreement with a manufacturing firm owned by Walter Selck. The Selck organization produced the rims.

During the period when the church controlled the patents, the licenses brought in several million dollars. This initiated a period of prosperity for the organization. The church paid off debts on existing property, acquired new properties, and built Founder's Church. It was income from the patents that made possible the building of Founder's Church, as about two thirds of the cost was paid from these funds.

CHAPTER VIII

I've Got A Big Pot Of Stew

The three decades after his return to Los Angeles in 1925 were rich and full for Holmes. These were the years of his lecturing and teaching through the Institute, and the years of his marriage to Hazel Foster. He was happy and fulfilled, both in his work and in his marriage.

Holmes' professional success cannot be attributed solely to the fact that he was a good speaker and an effective practitioner. He was also warm, kind, humorous, generous, earthy and highly gregarious. At the office he was always accessible, easy to reach and available.

Those who knew him well, through close personal and professional associations, had high praise of him. Reginald Armor remembered him as radiating "warmth, sureness and certainty." He left others "with a feeling of well-being and uplift, even though few words were spoken. One's inner reaction usually was 'here is a great man.'"

William Hart considered him to be a very loving person. "I have never known a human being," recalled Hart, "who loved other human beings more." Vetura Papke saw him in the same light. "He just loved people," recalled Vetura Papke. "He didn't care who they were. They were his biggest joy, and his real interest."

Shirley McAlpine recalled that on a personal level, one-on-one, "he gave out a great deal of love." Holmes seemed to be the kind of person people enjoyed being around. Jack Addington remembered him as "just a peach of a person to be with and a tremendous amount of fun."

Reginald Armor also saw him as being "happy, spontaneous, uninhibited and admitting of no limitation. . . . He bubbled with enthusiasm." It was characteristic of him, says Armor, to throw his arms around people, men and boys as well as women. He asked Armor, "How are you going to show love if you don't touch people." He liked being informal, and when he wasn't at the office he dressed causally. "Ernest, who had a nice wardrobe," William H. D. Hornaday remembers, "much preferred loafers and a sports jacket."

Robert Stack remembered that Holmes "didn't pretend anything. I never knew anyone who was more himself. He had less pretense than anyone I've ever known. He was totally unconcerned about 'image,' yet in his own way he had all he needed, and then some." Stack saw Holmes as a man without affectations. "He didn't play the saint or pastor. He didn't look like what you might expect such a magnetic personality to look like."

Reginald Armor described him as having wavy brown hair, "a little bit of plumpness, not fat, just pleasingly, moon faced, the grownup cherubic look of a choir boy." Holmes was a pipe smoker and carried Edgeworth tins in his pocket. Though not attracted to cigarettes, he also smoked two or three cigars a day. According to Armor he had practitioners treat for him to quit smoking, but it didn't work. Smoking brought him much pleasure, and in addition, he found it helped in his work. Much of his thinking was done with a pipe in his mouth.

He was not attracted to alcohol. One time at a party he was singing off tune (he was tone deaf) and the story was circulated that he was drinking heavily. Reginald Armor states emphatically that it was pure rumor. "I have never known him to take more than a glass or two of wine. In fact," said Armor, "anyone who knew Ernest realized that he was almost a teetotaler. He did not like 'the stuff' as he used to put it, but he would hasten to add that he had no objection to others taking a drink now and then if they so wished. That was their business. He had no patience, however, with over-indulgence."

Though Holmes was not an athlete, Bill Lynn remembers him as loving the out-doors. When on a vacation trip to the Pacific Northwest with Hazel and Lynn (who had just graduated from college), he enjoyed fishing in the ocean. He also liked to garden, harkening back to his boyhood days on a farm in rural Maine. Hazel often remarked, "I've never seen a person love the smell of manure the way he does."

When he and Hazel traveled, they never stayed in a hotel in the outskirts. He wanted to be downtown in the center of things. He told Reginald Armor, "On my visitations, lectures and travels, the busiest spot in the business part of town suits me fine. . . . I want to be in the middle of the activities of life." When he walked, which he loved to do with Hazel, he preferred walking on the sidewalks of a busy big city street. "That's where the action is," he said, "and I love action."

He and Hazel lived well, but, according to Bill Lynn, "not extravagantly." They always had a nice large house as well as a cook-housekeeper and a driver-handyman. There were always people in their home. "There was always room for more people at the Hill," (their home in the Palms area southwest of Beverly Hills) Reginald Armor remembers, "because Ernest and Hazel loved to entertain." They had many celebrity friends, who were always dropping by unexpectedly.

Holmes had a habit of inviting people at the last minute to dinner. Lena, the cook, had standing instructions to prepare enough food for the evening meal to serve at least three guests. Holmes himself loved to cook and Robert Bitzer remembers dropping in on Saturday afternoon and seeing him with a roast in the oven and a ham boiling on top of the stove.

Holmes was serious about his role as host and took great care in serving his guests. After a Sunday lecture he would invite eight or ten people saying, "Come on home with me and have dinner. I've got a big pot of stew just waiting." Elaine St. Johns recalls being at the Holmeses one evening for dinner, when the phone rang. Ernest was dishing out the beans to those seated around the table. The phone rang and rang and rang, and Ernest paid no attention to it. "I was going slowly mad," Elaine recalls, and finally said, "Ernest, answer the phone!" Holmes turned to her and said, "It's taken care of." The phone continued to ring and ring. Elaine grew more and more impatient, and finally said, "Ernest, answer the phone, it might be somebody who needs you!" Ernest again turned to her, and this time said, "Elaine, there are no cosmic problems," and went right on serving dinner.

The Holmeses enjoyed wide social contact, and during the course of their lifetime developed friendships with Norman Vincent Peale, famed for his writings on positive thinking, Nona Brooks, co-founder of the International Divine Science Association, Eileen Garrett, the noted English psychic, the Mahareshi Mahesh Yogi, creator of Transcendental Meditation, Goodwin Knight, the Governor of California, Dr. Robert Millikin, President of Cal Tech, the businessman J. Paul Getty, the astronomer Dr. Gustaf Stromberg, the philosopher Dr. Stephen Tornay and a host of movie stars including Peggy Lee, Robert Stack, Cary Grant, Mickey Rooney, Shelly Parker and figures from the silent movies Olive Thomas, Jack Pickford, Milton Sills and Doris Kenyon. In addition there was Hazel's lifelong friend, who also became a friend of Ernest, the pioneer woman reporter and author, the "mother confessor of Hollywood," Adela Rogers St. Johns.

For the most part the church became their social existence and their social circle revolved around it. They did not have, according to Bill Lynn, an intimate set of outside friends. Lynn observed that Ernest's closest friends were businessmen who he brought onto the

Board of Trustees, people like Lem Brumson, the first President of the Institute and Bill Haughey, who was President and general manager in the 1930s and 1940s.

Holmes liked to have family around. While he and Hazel had no children of their own (both were in their forties when they married), Holmes's mother and father, and two or three of his brothers and their families lived with them on and off during the early years of their marriage. He liked having family around at the office too. His mother and several relatives worked there.

Anna Holmes, his mother, became an institution in her own right at the office. At the time she came to California after raising her family in Maine she had not been acquainted with New Thought ideas. The more she read, the more interested she became and during her later years involved herself deeply in Religious Science, becoming herself a practitioner, working out of an office in the Institute. She was also the founder, and leader for twenty years of a welfare group, a volunteer organization which distributed clothes to the poor. She was ninety eight years old when she died, and active almost to the end. Elaine St. Johns described her as "one of a powerful group of women who worked at the Institute." Holmes, who according to Bill Lynn was not particularly close to any of his brothers, was devoted to his mother and close to her throughout her lifetime.

Reginald Armor, though a Religious Science minister and an Institute employee during his long career, was also like family to Holmes. Armor had been a member of Holmes' boy scout troop, when Holmes, as a young man in his twenties, was a scoutmaster in Venice shortly after arriving in California. Though fifteen years apart in age the two became friends, and Armor worked closely with Holmes throughout his entire career.

"Ernest had been like a father to me," Armor wrote, "perhaps psychologically he did replace my own father, for my stepfather and I were never close. . . . I know I always felt just like one of Ernest's own flesh and blood." Armor became a practitioner, and then a minister of Religious Science, and held positions of major responsibility throughout his long career at the Institute. He was known for his loyalty to Holmes, his versatility, and his willingness to do what needed to be done.

For a man who enjoyed people and thrived on wide personal contact, Holmes was also remarkably bookish. Bill Lynn recalled that he was always "surrounded by a stack of books. . . . He bought books ferociously." He scanned most of them, digging deeply into only a few. An important part of Holmes's life was spent with book in hand.

Holmes also took a personal interest in psychic abilities. While Hazel was more noted for her clairvoyance than he was, Holmes could, according to George Bendall, get flashes about where somebody had been at times in the past. He didn't make a big thing of it, telling Bendall, "Don't talk about it too much, George, people will not understand."

The most active decades of Holmes's professional career, the 1930s and 1940s, were decades of economic depression and world war. In his Sunday talks during World War II Holmes expressed his strong support for the American war effort. He had great faith in American democracy. "We believe in America," he told his congregation, "and in what it stands for. We believe that democracy is a spiritual idea, and that it is the destiny of this great nation to prove to the world that freedom under law and individual initiative under divine guidance is the right way to live."

Holmes felt it was possible to prosecute the war effort to its fullest, and at the same time maintain an attitude of peacefulness. "You and I, every person, every American, every freedom loving person throughout the world," he told his Sunday listeners, "is going to do everything he can do to crush despotism." At the same time, he pointed out, one doesn't "have to hate anyone to do it. We can keep calm and peaceful within, and have abiding trust and unilateral faith that right is might."

CHAPTER IX

He Was Not A Detail Man

Holmes often said that he preferred working solo, without an organization around him. In a moment of frustration over difficulties at the Institute, Holmes told Elaine St. Johns that he might have been better off had he never organized a Religious Science movement. Administration and organization were not his forte. Since he was primarily interested in philosophy and teaching, managerial tasks were of secondary concern. Consequently, he did not maintain full awareness of administrative matters at the Institute. Since a part of him wanted nothing to do with managing, he never fully paid attention to the details of the job.[1]

Nevertheless, he made his presence felt during his thirty years as Dean of the Institute. "Ernest was the central, solar body around which everything in the Institute evolved," said Reginald Armor. "It was his will in the teachings as to which way, which direction to go. He just didn't want to be bothered with details. He was not a detail man. He wanted to do his thing, which was to talk about God, the Infinite, the Absolute."

His problem as an administrator, Bill Lynn observed, was that he had a sense of mission, "but no idea of how to accomplish it through organization." He tended to shoot from the hip. If someone came to him with a proposal or suggestion which he responded favorably toward, he might say, "go do it," never bothering to explore the pros and cons or checking with others who might be affected. Carleton Whitehead felt that he did not follow through and delegated too much, shifting responsibility to others when he should have assumed it himself. Jack Addington saw the same weakness. "He was a loose administrator, wanting someone else to take the responsibility."

Reginald Armor observed that "Ernest would accept no limitation to his own spontaneous individuality," and as a result, tended to by-pass rules and regulations he himself established for administering the Institute. Craig Carter observed that if someone came into his office and wanted to teach or organize a church Holmes would, if he liked the person and thought there was a good chance of success, give his blessing without going through the Church Council, the group he set up to deal with such matters.

On the plus side, several people who worked for Holmes reported that there was a relaxed atmosphere at the office. He loved to laugh and joke with the staff, and in his one-on-one relationships he was generous, kind, warm and informal. Fletcher Harding recalls that his office door was always open." Vetura Papke remembers that she never heard anyone complain about working for him. "That's saying a lot," she emphasized, "for there were many, many people on the staff. He was not someone people were griping about."

Fletcher Harding considered him "swell to work for. I don't know how you could find anyone nicer. If my kids wanted to go fishing for a couple of days, no question, I could go." Holmes handled himself well in meetings and was willing to listen. Craig Carter recalls a staff meeting called for the purpose of deciding upon a name for a new church hymnal. Ernest let the discussion go on for twenty or thirty minutes until everyone had their say. Then someone asked his opinion. He said, "The only thing it can possibly be called is the Religious Science hymnal." By the time he spoke everyone was satisfied that the subject had been fully explored.

Holmes was supportive of his staff and his ministers. "Ernest would to go to bat for you," Craig Carter remembered. "He was very generous with his time, and he was always willing to go into small obscure churches." When Jack Addington started a church in San Diego Holmes told him, "Remember now, I'll come down and do anything I can." And he did, Addington commented. "He came down and spoke." When Addington's wife was ill, Holmes made a special trip to San Diego to visit her and treat for her. When Mrs. Addington died, Holmes officiated at the memorial services and brought Hazel and a crowd of people with him.

While there are many positive things to report about the manner in which Holmes handled his role as Dean of the Institute, he had weaknesses that hampered the growth of the Religious Science movement. Jack Addington felt that he attracted people who were too ambitious, "ministers who would get their start under him, get their feet solidly on the ground and then leave." Dealing with the difficult behavior of some of his ministers was his "greatest challenge," according to Vetura Papke. "Many moved away from the teaching and many broke his heart."

Bill Lynn believes that in his desire for harmony he acquiesced in a lot of things he should not have. Jack Addington confirms this observation, stating that "Ernest would do anything to be conciliatory." He did not have the ability to express anger, says Lynn. "I saw him angry only two or three times in my life."

Those who knew him generally agree that he was far too trusting. As Vetura Papke noted, "He saw only the goodness in everyone." He looked for the best in people, Jack Addington observed, "and in so doing overlooked faults." Bill Lynn says that Ernest did not believe that a person could do anything except that which was "good, proper, in harmony and progressive." He could be totally blinded by their shortcomings. It was the magnanimous part of his personality that got him in trouble. "In dealing with people he was generous, loving and *blinded.*"

Fletcher Harding felt that Holmes was "too permissive to be business like. We were his children. He loved us and was generous. It was like family." Holmes apparently viewed the Institute as a family enterprise, given the number of relatives that were on the payroll. The issue of nepotism was annoying to staff members during the years when the Institute was short of money.

On occasion Holmes did not respect the authority he granted to those who worked directly under him. During the last years of his life he developed a personal friendship with the young minister, George Bendall, who he had invited to live in his house after the death of Hazel. Bendall was also on the staff of William H. D. Hornaday, a top aid of Holmes at the time at the Institute. Hornaday and Bendall did not get along, and Hornaday wanted to fire Bendall. "He couldn't fire me," says Bendall "because of the special relationship I had with Ernest, even though he tried at least a half dozen times. It was a strange situation. I'd come home and Ernest would say, 'God, is he off again.' Ernest would then pick up the phone, call Hornaday and say, 'Bill, I am still alive. Be a good boy. George will be back to work in the morning.'"

On other occasions something would happen at the office or in the Religious Science movement that Holmes wanted to know about. He would tell Bendall, "Go check up on that and come back and tell me." After Bendall reported back to Holmes the two would discuss the matter, and Holmes would say, "I think it ought to be this way. Go tell 'em I said so." It's not surprising that Bendall was unpopular with his superiors at the office. "Everyone at headquarters," he remembers, "was afraid I wanted to be the Bishop or the Pope."

Holmes reportedly had difficulty working with strong leaders whom he brought into the Institute. Fletcher Harding observed that people like Stanley Bartlett, Joseph Murphy, Fredrick Bailes, Dan Custer and J. Lowry Fendrich, capable individuals who could have succeeded him as head of the Institute, never stayed long. Harding believed that Holmes was uncomfortable with them, "offended them in one way or another, or crowded them out." Part of the problem, according to George Bendall, lay in Holmes's propensity to become enamored with each for a period of time, telling them that they were going to be the next leader, and then becoming disenchanted and withholding his final blessing.

Holmes never chose a successor or set up a system of succession for himself as leader of the Religious Science movement. Several observers felt that this omission was one of the major mistakes of his career. George Bendall saw it as a major error because it left the choice of successor up "for power grabs." Bill Lynn said it was responsible "for the confusion the movement has been in since his time." Vetura Papke believes that the movement suffered, not only because he failed to appoint a successor, but because "he did not set up a system for approving or disapproving of additions to the teaching, or for providing direction for the movement."

CHAPTER X

We Called Her The Duchess

H_{azel} Holmes was an

extremely important figure in Holmes' life and a powerful presence in his work. She was much more than the beautifully dressed, attractive, well-connected socialite, much more than the devoted wife who was a charming hostess and managed the affairs of the Holmes household. Her skill as a practitioner was recognized soon after she became associated with the Institute and her reputation continued with a large clientele throughout the thirty years of her practice. Probably more important than her practitioner work was the role she played as a confidante and partner of Holmes in the expanding work of the Institute. As Adela Rogers St. Johns observed, "she became as much a part of the Science of Mind movement as Ernest himself."[1]

Hazel and Ernest were married in 1927, the same year the Institute was founded. Belonging to the social life of Los Angeles, Hazel, according to Fletcher Harding, "knew everybody who was anybody." She entertained the right people and introduced Ernest to the people who could help him. Elaine St. Johns termed her "a catalyst for Ernest because she was a very, very well-known gal in Hollywood." Fletcher Harding saw her as "the power behind the scenes. The movement would have been a lot less without her. It would have had trouble attracting the quality following and the money following."

Holmes grew to rely on her, not just for her contacts, but for her wise counsel. Bill Lynn said that she had a very strong personality, a fine mind and was very intuitive. It was she that Holmes talked to when he had a problem at work to solve. In the evening at dinner, according to Lynn who observed them in conversation, "Holmes would relate a problem to her, and she might say, 'I don't feel good about that. That doesn't sound right.'" Lynn says that Holmes relied heavily on Hazel's sense of the situation. She was his practitioner and "ultimate support for him" and a "very strong support." "She's my strength," Ernest once said about Hazel. "She has made our home such a place of peace that when I enter it, I immediately become calm."

Reginald Armor said that Holmes always had an inner circle, a special group of dedicated workers who met with him each week. Hazel was a member of this group. Admittance was by invitation only. Holmes would "let his hair down and explore a problem, knowing that he would not be misunderstood." Hazel, who usually sat towards the rear of the conference room, would now and then in a loud voice say, "Now, Papa, you know that isn't right." Holmes, who always respected her judgment, would, said Armor, "retrace his steps and look at the question from a different angle."

An indication of the influence she exercised is contained in a story Jack Addington tells about an effort he was involved in to upgrade *Science of Mind* magazine. Sometime in the late 1940s, when Fletcher Harding was in charge of the Ministry of Education, Addington and Harding, believing that the magazine had fallen on hard times, organized a committee to improve it. They held a meeting one evening at the home of a Religious Science minister in Pasadena who was also interested in helping out. Several people were invited, including Ernest and Hazel.

The group talked about changes that should be made. Harding, according to Addington, was coming on very strong because he felt he knew what needed to be done. At first Ernest and Hazel sat quietly on the side listening. As the meeting progressed Addington noticed that Hazel was squirming in her chair. Evidently, after she could stand it no longer, she turned to Ernest, and, in a voice loud enough for everyone to hear, said, "Ernest, you are not planning on giving these *boys* our magazine, are you?" The group fell silent, Addington recalls. "All of us kind of shrunk in our chairs."

Asked whether Hazel exerted more influence than she has been credited with, Addington said, "Oh, you said it. I am sure of it." Addington viewed Hazel as a powerful figure in the movement, playing an active role. She was interested in what was going on and kept herself informed. "She would come up to you," Addington recalls, "and say, 'what do you think about this.'" Addington knew that when she made up her mind on a question her views would carry weight with Holmes.

There was something majestic about Hazel, and there is no doubt that she exuded a strong personal presence. "She was always so regal," William H. D. Hornaday recalled, "that we affectionately called her 'the Duchess.'" When asked whether Hazel could be considered a co-partner of Holmes in facilitating the growth and development of the Religious Science movement, Bill Lynn replied, "I think Hazel was all of that."

Yet Hazel was not an out-front type person like Ernest. She was content to stay behind the scenes. "I don't recall," related Reginald Armor, "of ever hearing her speak out on any subject. She left the speaking to Ernest and discreetly stayed in the background as his conscience and his confidante." Elaine St. Johns pointed out that Hazel "never made a speech, never taught a class, and while she supported Ernest in every way, her main function was as a practitioner." Asked once why she kept herself backstage out of the limelight, she said, "People aren't interested in me. It is Ernest they want to hear from. I will not keep him away from anyone who wants to talk with him who he might be able to help."

The Hollywood columnist Adela Rogers St. Johns wrote the following description of Hazel at about the time she met Ernest: *"Hazel Gillan Foster, an elegant, wealthy young widow, was a native Californian. With the worlds of society, the powerful women's clubs, and the prestigious music circles open to her, Hazel moved graciously round the fringes while remaining a very private person. When she and her mother built one of the first luxury apartment houses near the Ambassador Hotel the elite of Hollywood knocked at her door. Her tenant-friends included such luminaries as Mabel Norman, Mary Pickford's brother, Jack, and his Follies star wife, and even the great D. W. Griffith himself."*

Reginald Armor gives us a picture of Hazel from the point of view of a family friend: *"A man could not help noticing that Hazel was beautiful of face and form. She had the peaches and cream complexion of the true redhead, and her auburn hair shone in the afternoon sun, just as did her open, warm generous nature. But the most impressive thing about Hazel was the very piercing eyes of the clairvoyant, the inner vision that sees not only the exterior but looks right through a man. She was not only lovely to see, gracious and charming to know, but every bit the gentle woman."*

Elaine St. Johns remembered Hazel as "a very sophisticated woman, attractive, and well dressed. She had studied music in Paris and it showed. Hazel and her mother had money, not with a capital M, but they were well fixed. They owned a very beautiful apartment building in Los Angeles. She was very much into music and Chinese art. . . . Everything around Hazel was beautiful." Bill Lynn remembers her "as the lady of the manor. . . . She never went anywhere in the daytime without a hat and gloves. . . . You could not picture Hazel making a bed. She could pull together a meal if she had to and she could rinse off the dishes on the maid's day off, but housework was other people's work."

Like Ernest, Hazel was outgoing and generous. Reginald Armor tells the story of how Hazel would give away a corsage she was wearing to the first person who admired it. "Beads, the same way," he recalled. "Hats—if someone admired her hat, she would take it off and say, 'It's yours.' Rings and jewelry—the same way."

Armor related how Hazel and Ernest met. Hazel's Aunt Gussie, who Ernest had known since his first days in Venice as a Scoutmaster, introduced them. Gussie Rundell, a Los Angeles resident, had become a fan of Ernest's after his return from the East coast in 1925, attending his lectures, and coming to him for practitioner work. The scene Armor described below was in Ernest's practitioner office in Los Angeles:

"Aunt Gussie showed up one morning at Ernest's practitioner office with Hazel physically in tow. It was obvious that there had been words of discussion in getting her to the door. 'I told her she needs to talk to a practitioner,' said Gussie, as she deposited Hazel on Holmes' doorstep. . . . Fortunately, Ernest had some open time on his schedule. Always interested in solving the problems of others, he kindly invited Hazel into the office and closed the door. Normally he was able to diagnose a case in fifteen or twenty minutes. This time, however, it was nearly an hour before the door opened. Hazel's demeanor was entirely different when she came out from when she went in. Hazel commented, "I wasn't aware that Ernest and I had met before. But do you know, he told me I was the second person he met when he first came to California and landed in Venice many years ago. Isn't that amazing. And he remembered me all those years.'"

Armor remembers that Hazel immediately involved herself in Religious Science, "learning, studying and listening to Holmes, the lecturer, and seeing Holmes, the man." Elaine St. Johns, Adela Rogers St. Johns' daughter, remembers that when it was known that her mother's good friend Hazel was interested in a preacher, and a metaphysical one at that, "there was a stampede to take a look at him." Evidently the social group around Hazel approved because, as Adela Rogers St. Johns testified, Hazel threw herself into the Religious Science movement, establishing a niche for herself as a practitioner.

Married soon after they met, they were together for thirty years until Hazel's death in 1957. Several who knew them saw their marriage as reaching a high level of marital companionship and love. Bill Lynn says, "I never had the privilege of observing such a deep and respectful love affair between two people as between Hazel and Ernest. I really never witnessed a cross word." Adela Rogers St. Johns called their thirty-year marriage, "a perfect partnership physically, mentally and spiritually. I call that a superior demonstration of universal love particularized." Omar Fareed, the Holmes' physician and family friend, called it, "one of the great friendships." Fletcher Harding viewed their relationship as "a rich companionship."

Ernest and Hazel not only enjoyed each other, but socialized well as a couple, enjoying each other's family and friends. They loved to entertain, and their home was usually bustling with activity. After they married, Hazel went to live with Ernest and his family on "The Hill" in Palms, and from all reports got on well with his mother and father, and his brothers.

Reginald Armor noted that Hazel had highly developed psychic abilities, "a diagnostic clairvoyance comparable to Quimby's" (the 19th century founder of the New Thought movement). Elaine St. Johns told of how Hazel and Ernest would be out for a drive and Hazel would say, "Ernest, you'd better look at the right front tire," and sure enough there would be a leak or nail in it. Elaine St. Johns also tells a story about the canned food of all kinds that Ernest loved to stock in the pantry. One year mice got in and ate all the labels off the cans. "Ernest would pick up a can and shake it to see if he could get an idea of what might be in it, and then would ask Hazel, who simply knew what was in the can."

Hazel's acquaintance with psychic phenomena and her ability as a clairvoyant may have led Ernest to believe that he could make contact with her through the use of a medium after she died. Reginald Armor says that Holmes tried on several occasions to establish "conscious contact." Though he felt that a connection of some kind was made, he was never quite convinced that it was actually Hazel who was speaking to him.

It is not surprising that Hazel's death had a deep impact on Holmes. Elaine St. Johns observed that "Ernest's life was very empty after Hazel. He didn't know what to do with himself after she died. Something in his heart of hearts was gone. After she went Ernest wanted to go too. He wanted to join her. He never had a doubt that Hazel was waiting for him."

CHAPTER XI

There Is Something Wrong With Our Set-Up

T he decade of the 1940s was a period of rapid growth in the Religious Science movement. Thirty-nine new congregations established themselves. There were seven in existence in 1940 and forty-six in 1950.[1] Fletcher Harding described the decade of the 1940s as an exciting period of growth in the movement.

As the number of congregations grew (they were first called branches of the Institute, and then, in 1942, chapters) the leaders, particularly in Los Angeles, began meeting informally to discuss common problems. They asked for and received permission in 1942 from the Institute to organize formally as a group. Called the Religious Science Chapter Association, the group began holding regular meetings and an annual conference to focus on issues of mutual concern. Holmes supported their work, attending their conferences and often gave the closing address. He saw their efforts in alignment with the goals of the Institute.

Five years later in 1947, representatives of the Chapter Association met with Holmes and suggested that, since the movement was undergoing such rapid growth the responsibilities of the Chapter Association be expanded to include management of the churches. They recommended that a new non-profit association be organized for this purpose. Holmes, who was now in his sixties and had been considering retirement, agreed to a proposal by Robert Bitzer, then head of the Southern California Chapter Association, to create a committee to study the matter and make suggestions.[2]

The Committee charged with responsibility for proposing a new organizational plan was composed of ministers who were respected in the movement. Included among them were Carmelita Trowbridge of Alhambra, Dan Custer of San Francisco, and Wayne Kintner of Rochester, NY In the spring of 1948 the committee submitted a proposed constitution for a new organization, to be called the International Association of Religious Science Churches (IARSC).

The constitution conferred upon the proposed new organization several powers that were currently being performed by the Institute. The IARSC would have the power to grant and rescind charters for chapters (which were now to be called churches), suspend or expel for just cause a church leader or minister, maintain the integrity of the teaching as set forth in *The Science of Mind* textbook, appoint and send out lecturers, and establish general standards of procedure, ethics, methods and ideals for the churches and church leaders.[3]

The proposed shift in administrative authority from the Institute to a new group was opposed by some members of the Institute's Board. Arion Lewis, a member of the Board of Trustees and the Institute's legal counsel, raised strong objections to the proposed new organization.

Voicing his objections in a letter to Holmes, he wrote, "I do not believe it wise for the Board of Trustees of the Institute to surrender the powers and prerogatives which they now have, which would be exactly what would happen under the proposed constitution which I have before me. I wish to point out at this time that the enumerated powers of the Congress are so all inclusive that the adoption of these provisions would in a real sense mean a complete surrender or abdication by the Institute and its Board of most of the powers and prerogatives which they now enjoy, and. . . . in a real sense make the Institute of Religious Science and Philosophy a mere ward of the international organization. The problem or question is, broadly speaking, whether or not the Institute desires to create an over-all organization and become itself subordinate to that organization."[4]

Support for the proposed new IARSC came from associates Holmes liked and respected. Charles Kinnear, a minister on the Institute's staff, drafted a memorandum which argued that the Institute's Board of Trustees would continue to be the parent authority and would still be ultimately responsible for providing guidance and direction to the movement.

In addition, it was asserted that the new plan had within it a clear-cut division of authority and responsibility between the Institute and the new organization. Dan Custer lauded the constitution of the new group. It was, he said "a constitution for democratic government." He considered it to be "the greatest thing that ever happened to us." Raymond Charles Barker, who was one of Holmes' most trusted associates, a man who some thought might someday succeed him as Dean of the Institute, praised the proposed constitution as "a new democratic form of government for the Religious Science Movement."[5]

Holmes agreed to the creation of the IARSC, despite the fact that it would mean reduced authority for the Institute. There were several apparent reasons for doing so. First, the teaching function, which he was most interested in and committed to, remained in the Institute. Ministerial and practitioner training would still be under its control. Secondly, for several years he had let it be known that he wanted to step down as Dean of the Institute and head of the movement.

He had been so far unsuccessful in his efforts to groom a successor to himself. He had failed to select the obvious candidates, Robert Bitzer of the Hollywood church, or Raymond Charles Barker, leader of the large congregation in New York City. Younger ministers who had worked with him at the Institute, talented men like Frederick Bailes, Stanley Bartlett, J. Lowry Fendrich and Fletcher Harding, were all found wanting for one reason or another.[6] By turning over management of the churches to the IARSC, primary responsibility for guiding the Movement in the future would rest with the new group and there would be no need to choose a successor.

It appears that the principal reason for his agreeing to the formation of the IARSC was his desire to create an organization which would preserve his work. "I have put twenty-five years and a fortune of money into this teaching," he told a meeting of ministers. "It must be preserved." He had come to the conclusion that the current organizational structure of the Institute was not adequate to handle the job of the rapidly expanding church movement. "I have come to the positive, absolute, final conclusion," he told the ministers. "We have reached a point, we have reached a horizon of growth under our present method. It is impossible for us to arrive at our goal," he said, under the current organizational arrangements.[7]

Holmes had decided, as Fletcher Harding reported, "that he wanted to leave the movement as a spiritual democracy." He felt that the Religious Science movement would benefit if it were organized in a manner similar to that of the Government of the United States. "In the name of individual and collective freedom," he told the ministers, we shall develop a system "patterned after the Constitution the United States", and expressing hope for the new system that he was about to approve, he said, "We have arrived at the first beginning of the most democratic spiritual organization the world has ever known."

The International Association of Religious Science Churches (IARSC) began functioning on January 5, 1949, when the constitution and by-laws were adopted by the annual conference of Religious Science Churches meeting in convention in Los Angeles. A review of its organizational structure shows that Holmes's wish that the group function on a democratic basis had been carried out. Ultimate authority rested in the Congress of Religious Science Churches which would meet annually each January. The Congress had the power to decide upon church policies and procedures, to make directives and determine the organization's budget. At the annual Congress each church was represented by its minister and a voting delegate for each fifty church members.

A Representative Council, comprised of eleven members (seven ministers and four laymen) were elected by the membership at its annual meeting. Holmes was appointed as a life member of the Council. He was not, however, accorded the expansive powers of Permanent Trustee that he possessed as a member of the Board of Trustees of the Institute of Religious Science and Philosophy. The Representative Council was headed by a President who was elected by the membership at its annual meeting.

The Council itself was assigned executive responsibility for managing the affairs of the IARSC. The President, as chairman of the Council, was the organization's chief executive officer. He was to be assisted by an Executive Secretary. Office space was provided for the organization in the Institute's headquarters in Los Angeles.

Under the new arrangement the IARSC was considered "The Church organization" The Institute was the school. It was responsible for the education of ministers and for providing the curriculum for the Science of Mind courses. The churches, through their accredited ministers and teachers were to "teach and proclaim this philosophy to the world."

Officials of the IARSC spoke of the organization's mission in glowing terms. "It is our vision and our prayer," stated Fletcher Harding, the organization's first President, "that through the democratic organization the teachings of Religious Science may be carried to the far corners of the world as well as spread abroad in our land."[8]

From the outset there was difficulty in the relationship between the Institute and the IARSC, and these difficulties continued throughout the five-year period (1949-1954) that the two organizations attempted to work together. Territorial disputes were continually erupting. Under the existing organizational arrangements, no one, including Holmes, had the authority to resolve these disagreements.

Credentialing became a major stumbling block. Each church organization was required to apply to the IARSC for a charter to operate and apply to the Institute for a charter to teach. Each chartering body had certain, definite functions, but there was an overlapping of authority. Given the way the organizations were set up, Fletcher Harding later surmised, "it was inevitable that there would be a clash between Ernest and the IARSC over the issue of credentialing."

Within a short time the Representative Council became dissatisfied with the educational program of the Institute, considering it weak and ineffectual, and unable to furnish the type of minister who could go out and succeed. The Council was also displeased by the rapid turnover of educational administrators at the Institute. Whenever a new director of education came in, according to Council reports, there was "a complete turnover of educational policy." As a result, the churches were left in confusion about what to teach and when to teach it. [9]

The IARSC was evidently openly critical of several Institute practices. Bill Lynn recalled that the IARSC kept "telling the Institute what to do and making demands upon it." It is not surprising, that in the process, Institute officials became disenchanted with the new group.

There were petty problems. The IARSC was not satisfied with the office space it had been provided and, without telling Holmes, rented office space outside the Institute building. Jack Addington recalled that Holmes was annoyed. "He did not like what they did and he told them so."

Addington said that Holmes, from the beginning, "did not like the IARSC." That dislike grew, as Carleton Whitehead observed, as the IARSC assumed the prerogatives previously enjoyed by the Institute. In 1953 Holmes came to the conclusion that it was "physically, intellectually and emotionally impossible" for the two organizations to function together with one purpose in mind. He decided that changes needed to be made. [10]

Leaders of the IARSC also recognized that the system was not working. The Representative Council diagnosed the problem as lying in "the natural conflict that arises when two organizations attempt to govern." Robert Bitzer of the Representative Council agreed with Holmes that changes needed to be made. "We cannot go on the way we have been in the past," he said. "There must be unification, and until there is one governing board, elected unanimously in the same way, and therefore having responsibility to the people, we'll not have a unity in our basic teaching, and there will be confusion."[11]

The Institute's Board of Trustees in 1953 devised a method called *The Plan* for combining the activities of both organizations. The Institute would change its name to the Church of Religious Science, revise its by-laws so that it would become the sole governing body for all Religious Science churches, and take over all the functions of the IARSC.

Holmes, and representatives of the Institute's Board, discussed *The Plan* with the IARSC's Representative Council in late 1953 and requested and received permission to present it to the delegates of the IARSC during its 5th annual Congress in Los Angeles, January 4-8, 1954. (This meeting has since been referred to as the "Split Meeting"). Holmes and the Institute's Board undoubtedly hoped that the Congress of the IARSC and its Representative Council would endorse *The Plan* and recommend that the individual churches adopt it.

The Plan which was contained in a lengthy fifty-two page document, had not been distributed to the churches before the Congress began. As a result the Institute's proposal took many delegates by surprise. Many were annoyed, not only because they had no opportunity to study and consider it beforehand, but because there was an apparent unwillingness by Holmes and the Institute's Board to accept modifications. The only way to obtain a copy of *The Plan* according to Carleton Whitehead, a minister who attended the Congress, "was for a minister to sign a statement saying that he/she would present *The Plan* to his/her congregation."

John Hefferlin, a minister from Long Beach and a member of the Representative Council, expressed a resentment shared by other delegates when he said, "I have reflexes. I don't like to be told to do this or else, and I have been told that." Hefferlin went on to say that in meetings of the Representative Council before the Congress began, the question was asked, "is there any possibility that we can go over with the Board of Trustees this proposition and suggest any possible changes or alterations?" The answer, Hefferlin said, was, "No, you must take it as it is, then after you are in you can make suggestions."[12]

Raymond Barker voiced similar criticism of the manner in which *The Plan* was presented and the uncompromising attitude of the Institute's Board. "It has been interesting to me," he said, "that in both the Council meetings and in discussions with officials of the Institute that they are completely adamant on every point of their plan, and will not make a change. I have been unhappy over what I call the autocratic method of presentation. They have said to us, 'You're either in or you're out.'"

Lora Holman, former President of the IARSC, corroborated his comments, saying, "We asked repeatedly in the Representative Council to Dr. Holmes, 'Will you even consider changes? Are we wasting our time to give them consideration? And we were told 'yes,' we were wasting our time because it couldn't be done."[13]

Ministers, who over a five-year period had developed a loyalty to the IARSC, were upset because *The Plan* if adopted by the churches, would result in the organization's complete demise. Raymond Barker was particularly bitter about the fact that the organization he now headed, and had devoted several years to build, would be put out of existence. "Do you realize," he told Craig Carter, "that they (referring to Holmes and the Institute Board) are using the floor of our own Congress to destroy us?" Indeed, Carter recalled, that is exactly what was happening. "Holmes," Carter confirmed, "was using the Congress to do away with the IARSC and set up a totally new system, and the old-timers resented it."

The key feature in The Plan that drew the most criticism was a provision relating to the composition of the Board of Trustees and the grant of personal power over membership on the Board to Holmes himself as Permanent Trustee. Holmes and others in establishing the IARSC in 1949 had made much over the fact that the new governing system for the church would be based on democratic principles. The Church by-laws that were now being proposed carried none of the democratic safeguards that were in the IARSC Constitution. They placed controlling power in the Institute's undemocratically elected, self-perpetuating Board.[14]

The new Board of Trustees of the Church of Religious Science was to be composed of eighteen members, but only seven were to be elected at an annual convention of member churches. The remaining eleven, comprising a majority, were to come from the Board of the Institute. As a result, the operations of the Church would be controlled by the Board members of the former Institute of Religious Science and School of Philosophy.

Under the new organizational arrangement, Ernest Holmes would still enjoy the rights he had long held as "Permanent Trustee." This trusteeship, in addition to giving him life tenure on the Board, also gave him the right to request and receive, without cause, the resignation of any one of the eighteen Board members.

Barker pointed out the undemocratic nature of the provision. "We asked the question of one of the Institute's lawyers who worked on *The Plan*, did Dr. Holmes's power as Permanent Trustee give him the power to ask for the resignation of any seven we elect, and the answer was 'yes'. We can elect seven members of the Board of Trustees, and at any time Dr. Holmes can say to any one of our newly elected members, 'we do not see eye to eye on this thing, and as Permanent Trustee, I ask for your resignation,' and that person is immediately out." Barker told the delegates that the proposed new arrangement was unsatisfactory. The Board was unbalanced and there were insufficient guarantees for a democratic system, and therefore he could not support it.[15]

Lora Holman, Minister from Glendale, whose term as President of the IARSC ended with the adjournment of the Congress, supported Barker's position. "The whole trend of thought," she told the delegates, "is moving towards the democratic government of things.... In the Religious Science movement a few years ago, Dr. Holmes recognized the principle and established the IARSC on that basis, on the basis of representative government, government by the consent of the governed. . . . the whole movement is toward representative government throughout the world, and to lose it is definitely taking a step backward toward the darkness of the ages, and I can't see it."

On the last day of the Congress, Friday, January 8, 1954, Holmes himself took the floor of the convention to defend *The Plan* and to explain his position. First, he made it clear that *The Plan* was not something he reluctantly agreed to after pressure from the Institute Board. It was a proposal that he himself initiated. "I solely and alone am responsible for *The Plan*," he said. He regretted that other Institute Board members were "taking the heat" for it, because it was he himself who was responsible for originating it. "It became evident to me a year ago," he said, "that something definite would have to be done. Last summer I determined to do it, to introduce some new kind of idea that would put the thing together. This is the idea."

He told the delegates that they should know that there is general agreement, both on the part of the Institute's Board, and the Representative Council, that a crisis point had been reached and the two organizations could not continue to function as they had been in the past. We all agree, he said, "it cannot exist the way it is. . . . there is something wrong with our set-up." The only way to avoid the trouble, he had concluded, was to have one final board. "The discord," he said, was not the result of "people fighting each other. . . . or disliking or hating each other." It was a disunity that results from there being no "final place of agreement" on where the authority rests.

Holmes then spoke to the question of the Permanent Trusteeship, which was being strongly criticized. He let it be known that he had no intention of giving it up. "This is undemocratic," he said. "I've never said it wasn't. Mr. Lewis, our attorney, has always said it was. He's never been for it. Jack Fostinis wasn't for it. Most of my board have not been for it. This is a strange situation, isn't it? Well, I just happen to be a purpose, a person who for twenty-five years has had only one purpose in mind. And I have known that unless that purpose was accomplished within such ability as I have, if I live, that purpose cannot be clouded by anyone.

"You can take the best thought and the best idea in the world and so twist it and reinterpret it, that it loses its entire validity and effectiveness. Therefore, I do not intend, and this is notice to Mr. Lewis as well as to you, to give up my Permanent Trusteeship in the interest of Religious Science. The purpose for which it exists is that I may not myself be thrown out by someone who doesn't know what that purpose is.

"That's what I believe. Now, that's undemocratic. No one knows it better than I do. That's autocratic. That's one hundred percent arbitrary."

Holmes then went on to speak in his own defense, to justify his right to have final say over the movement. "Let me tell you something, my friends," he said. "You do not know what life has been for twenty-seven years. You haven't the slightest concept. It's creating something out of nothing. It's financing that is keeping it going when Boards come and leave and get mad and go away and take their own, and have every legal and moral and ethical right apparently to think it, and you trust yourself when all men doubt you."

Holmes then restated his position on his power as Permanent Trustee. "I will be the deciding one because I have no intention of quitting what I started. That's out, if that's wrong, it remains wrong. I can't help it. You'd be in the same position."[16]

Holmes's unwillingness to give up his power as Permanent Trustee was a major sticking point. As the following exchange on the floor of the Congress indicates, it may have been an important factor in convincing some members to withhold support for *The Plan.* Jack Addington, who was personally close to Holmes, was presiding on the podium.

Addington: "The other day when I spoke, I spoke in behalf of unity. I'm still talking about unity, but there are a couple of questions I would like to ask.... Now I would like to ask Dr. Holmes a question, and it's a 'yes' or 'no' question. Would the Institute of Religious

Science Board of Trustees, be willing to sit down with representatives of this group and work out a plan that is acceptable to everyone along the lines that they have suggested. . . . Could we, Ernest?

Holmes: "I know of no reason why they would not."

Addington: "Well, do you think they would?"

Holmes: "I know of no reason why they would not, Jack."

Addington: "Well, what do you think Reg? (speaking to Reginald Armor). Would you as a member of the Board of Trustees be willing to work out a compromise plan?"

Armor: "Well, I don't think it would ever hurt to, ah, although it would be better, ah."

Addington: "But I mean, suppose some good suggestion came forward. Why couldn't we have a Board where we have representation without having a Permanent Trusteeship? When I went to San Diego I deliberately did away with a permanent trusteeship because we didn't want it. . . . I don't think anyone should have control of a Board. What the heck is a Board if anyone has control over it. . . . I'm for *The Plan* but I think some changes have to be made. . . . Let's get together and work it out. Now, Ernest said we can do it. For goodness sakes, let's get together and do it and let's quit playing around."

Voice from the audience: "Did his lawyer say we can do it? Get a statement from the lawyer."

Addington: "Alright, Arion, where are you Arion? Do you think we can do it or can't we?"

Arion Lewis: (the Institute's lawyer) "Well, there's lots of room for change in any good plan."

Addington: "Well, do you believe this change?" (referring to the points that were not acceptable to the Representative Council of the IARSC.).

Lewis: "And to the question you put specifically, the answer at the present is 'No.'"

Addington: "Well, then that settles it. That settles it. . . . If it's 'no,' then I'm with the IARSC 100 per cent" [17]

When interviewed in February 1991 Addington remembered the response of Arion Lewis to his questioning as being the turning point. It was now clear that a compromise solution was unacceptable to Holmes and the Board of Trustees of the Institute. It was at that moment that a split in the movement became inevitable.[18]

While the controversy over the composition of the new Board and the power of Holmes as Permanent Trustee were important issues, another equally important question was lying under the surface. It concerned the choice of Holmes' successor as leader of the movement. If *The Plan* were adopted the power to make that choice would no longer be in the hands of the IARSC. It would revert to the Board of Trustees of the Institute.

Holmes was now past sixty-five. Several who knew him believed his health was declining. He often talked about retirement. No one believed he would be around for long. Who would the Institute's Board appoint, or, on his retirement, who would Holmes himself choose? Many in the movement felt the heir apparent was Dr. William H. D. Hornaday.

A Californian in his early forties, Hornaday was the descendant of several generations of ministers, and was a Methodist minister himself before becoming ordained as a minister of Religious Science. He had joined the movement in the early 1950s, shared the speaker's platform with Holmes at the Wiltern on Sundays, and was a principal associate of Holmes at the Institute.

At the time *The Plan* was being developed at the Institute in 1953 Hornaday was in the thick of it and was considered the new "hot shot" in the movement.[19] Many ministers were reportedly concerned that, once *The Plan* was adopted, Holmes was going to turn the mantle of leadership over to Hornaday. Many of Hornaday's supporters, according to Bill Lynn, were already convinced that Holmes had already given Hornaday his blessing.

During the course of the split meeting George Bendall recalled seeing Holmes put his arm around Hornaday, and in front of a large group, practically anoint him on the spot, saying, "This will be the next head of the movement." This, Bendall believes, more than anything else, "was the straw that broke the camel's back." He sees it as "the emotional and motivating factor" behind the opposition of many ministers to The Plan.

The leaders of the IARSC, particularly the President and Vice President of the Representative Council, Raymond Barker and Robert Bitzer, had reason to believe that their credentials as longtime leaders of both the Religious Science and New Thought movements, qualified them to lead once Holmes was gone. They had every reason to view Hornaday as a "Johnny-come-lately."

The arguments offered by those who opposed *The Plan* made no mention of the possibility of the appointment of an unacceptable successor to Holmes, but focused on the issue of democracy in the movement. Lora Holman expressed her regret in opposing The Plan but felt an important principle was involved. "Regardless of how I might differ in matter of principle of government with Dr. Holmes," she said, "I shall always love him and be grateful to him for what he has given to the world, but I cannot put personalities above what seems to me to be the principle of freedom in this movement."

Raymond Barker encouraged the delegates to stick with the IARSC. "The IARSC is a separate corporation," he told them. "There isn't a thing this plan can do to it. There is no way of affecting us except perhaps taking some of our membership." Barker said that the question that the ministers must now individually decide was, "which organization do you want to be in. The IARSC I can assure you, from the opinions of the Council, will not disband."[20]

A majority of ministers appeared to be willing to go along with Holmes and the Institute Board. Ethel Barnhard, minister from the church in Santa Anita, CA, probably expressed the thinking of many when she said, "I believe in the teaching. I am giving my life to it. I would do anything for it. I believe in Ernest Holmes. I do not believe anybody is trying to ruin anything in this plan. I am sure this new plan has many, many things that need changing in it. I know it is better than we had."[21] Lornie Grinton, one of the newly ordained younger ministers reflected a similar view when he said, "I am staying with the man who gave me the understanding of my God and my spiritual life."

Craig Carter, who had been a strong supporter of Holmes, said, "I don't like to work under a divided command. . . . Someone suggested that we are faced with no alternative but to have two bodies. . . . We do not have to go on having an IARSC."

Irma Glen, who had been a member of the Representative Council, probably made the most eloquent statement of the position of those who decided to support the Holmes proposal. The Plan is not perfect," she said, "but Ernest Holmes has told us that changes will be made as we go on. . . . I cannot conceive of an organization operating independently of its Founder while he is still here with us. It would seem to me that members of Religious Science churches would have confidence in the founder of the movement and that they would be interested in the teachings of Religious Science as it emanates from its source."[22]

Before the Congress adjourned the members and delegates of the Congress passed a motion instructing their Representative Council to make a thorough study of The Plan and report back within forty-five days to all ministers and delegates.

In early February the Representative Council completed its report and sent it with a covering letter to member churches. The Council criticized the Institute as an autocracy, pointed with pride to the democratic nature of the IARSC's decision-making processes and to its organization's successes, argued that only a democratically led organization could ensure the continued expansion of the movement, deplored the fact that acceptance of *The Plan* by the churches would mean the demise of the IARSC, concluded that the Institute's plan was unacceptable, and announced its intention to continue to lead the Movement.[23]

"The new plan and by-laws," the Representative Council stated, "reserves administrative control and authority in the parent organization. This is in direct contradiction to the fundamental rule of determination of policies, organization, program and expansion by the member churches of the IARSC through the democratic process. . . . The IARSC was organized as a corporate body based upon democratic principles and practices of its member churches, with the full knowledge and cooperation of Dr. Holmes. . . . The IARSC has gone forward at every point to where it has been possible to break down autocracy and sustain a practice of democracy. . . . The democratic procedure the International has followed has shown the trustworthiness of the organization. . . . We believe that only a democratic organization can build a world-wide organization of Religious Science Churches. . . . The IARSC is a sound organization. . . . It is in sound financial condition. . . . If the 'New Plan" was accepted by the churches and they affiliated with the former Institute, now known as the 'Church of Religious Science,' this great democratic organization would no longer exist."[24]

After rejecting *The Plan* the IARSC, in what its leaders must have known was an effort doomed to fail, sent a letter on February 16, 1954 to the Institute's Board of Trustees proposing that the Institute turn over its teaching function to the IARSC. In this proposal the IARSC would further expand its functions at the expense of the Institute.

The letter stated, "The power and authority in the movement would be in the IARSC and would be completely controlled by member churches themselves. . . . The College of Religious Science will be a function of the IARSC with the member churches teaching accredited classes. The present college and those elsewhere will be a part of the International College of Religious Science." The IARSC's letter concluded by asserting, "We need one organization to bring unity into our movement and keep it unified. We feel that the destiny of a movement as great as this should be in the hands of the churches themselves—these are the people which make up the movement. We pray this may be accomplished."[25]

It came as no surprise when the Board of the Institute did not accept the proposal. The Institute's Board passed a resolution resigning from "any relationship with the IARSC", and moved to revoke all teaching chapters of any church that failed to affiliate with the new Church of Religious Science.

It took several weeks before each of the churches held a meeting of its board of directors to hear the pros and cons of adopting *The Plan*. As the churches voted and the results came in, it was apparent that sentiment was divided. While a majority adopted the Institute's plan, a sizable minority, including some of the movement's largest churches, and led by some of its strongest leaders, were remaining with the IARSC.[26]

CHAPTER XII

His Dream Was Not Coming True

Holmes was under a great deal of strain during the period of controversy that led to the split in the movement. The Split meeting, Bill Lynn noted, "was the culmination of one of the most trying periods in Ernest's life." Vetura Papke saw a big difference in Holmes after the split. "Sometimes he was so sad. His dream was not coming true." He was hurt, Frieda Grinton observed, "very hurt, you could see it, you could feel it when you were around him." Fletcher Harding noted that "Ernest was never the same after the fighting, quarreling and dissension that led to the split."[1]

Despite his disappointment, Holmes apparently did not hold a grudge against the ministers who left him. Vetura Papke said that Holmes maintained his friendship with all of them. "They called him and he called them." Holmes told Lornie Grinton, a loyal newly ordained minister, who was upset with those who left, that he was not going to separate himself from those who remained with the IARSC. "We all have our differences," he told Grinton. "We all have our own way of looking at things. You must bless and love those who have turned away. They believe they are right and I will not argue with them."

George Bendall remembered that Holmes considered the ministers who stayed with the IARSC as "still his people, and he didn't care what name they called it." He would go to their conventions and speak and lecture. As far as Holmes was concerned, said Bendall, they were still in the Movement.

Carleton Whitehead, who stayed with the International, said that the Split "didn't interrupt my relationship with him." When Holmes came to the annual church convention at Asilomar, he always invited Whitehead, who had a congregation in nearby Monterey, CA, to visit him at the convention. Jack Addington recalled that Holmes never held anything against him. "He'd call me, say from Palm Springs and say, 'I can be over there in a couple of hours. Let's have dinner tonight'." When Addington began building a church in San Diego, he says, Holmes "came down, went over the plans and made suggestions."

Holmes's relationship with Raymond Barker remained close, and shortly after the Split, Holmes traveled to New York to speak for him at his church. One of the last letters he wrote before he died in early 1960 was to Raymond Barker, expressing his belief that the sides would ultimately settle their differences. "I am sure your interest is in the permanency of the movement," Holmes wrote, "the same as mine is, even though we are on two sides of the same coin. Of course, I know the whole thing will come back together when the right time comes, because it is the logical thing to do, and I think, in the long run, common sense usually wins."

Carleton Whitehead believed that Holmes came to realize in his last years that he erred when he pushed *The Plan* for unification of the movement, and came to regret his decision. George Bendall agreed with this view. Holmes realized in 1958, according to Bendall, that he had made a mistake when he allowed the split to take place. "It was the one big thing on his mind" during the last months of his life.

In the six year period between the time of the split and his death (1954-1960), Holmes failed to confer the mantle of leadership on anyone. He evidently became disenchanted with William H. D. Hornaday, as he had with every other minister he had considered for the job. There are several explanations for his unwillingness to appoint Hornaday or any of the others before him. According to Bill Lynn, Holmes believed that the obvious successor, the perfect choice, would simply arise. One of the great frustrations of the last years of his life was that no one emerged who met all of his expectations.

Jack Addington believed that Holmes was concerned about choosing unwisely. While he recognized the need for a successor, no potential successor ever fully satisfied him. He felt that a poor choice would result in loss of membership and ministers.

Fletcher Harding took a different view. He maintained that Holmes was always threatened by stronger people who arose in the movement and would have been "terribly uncomfortable to see another strong individual rising to take his place during his life-time." George Bendall reported a conversation he had with Holmes during the last year of his life which supports Harding's view. Bendall and Holmes were discussing the current lack of leadership in the movement when Bendall said, "I think you set it up that way because when you died nobody was going to have it. You were going to take it with you." Bendall remembers that his comment made Holmes angry and that Holmes didn't speak to him for several days. Then he came to Bendall and said, "You're right."

CHAPTER XIII

I Want To Get With My Beloved

After the Split, Holmes took the view, according to Bill Lynn, that "It's up to somebody else. If the organization is worthy of survival it will survive." Fletcher Harding observed that Holmes was on the point of "hanging up his gloves" when Hazel died.[1]

Her death in 1957 had a major impact on him. "It was very, very hard on Ernest," recalls Frieda Grinton. "It was the first time I saw Ernest almost fall apart." For months after her passing, Reginald Armor saw him pacing up and down the hallway of his home saying to himself, "This is terrible. Just terrible." Bill Lynn believes that Holmes never allowed himself to think that Hazel would die before he did. When she left, it was a tremendous shock to his whole thinking process. After she was gone, Elaine St. Johns recalls, "Ernest wanted to go. He wanted to join her."

It was apparent to Vetura Papke that after Hazel's death, Holmes lost interest in the Institute and the movement. Lynn noted the same thing, and commented that after Hazel's death, "he felt that his life's work was done." People would tell him to write another book. Lynn recalls that Ernest would reply, "I've said everything I've got to say. Every time I try to write something, it's writing the same thing in different words. I've done it all."

With Hazel gone, he too was ready to go. He recognized that his life had been rich and full. Not long before he had commented to a large group of people, "The world has given me everything that it gives to most people and more, of pleasure and happiness and love and friendship and contentment and intense activity, which is life to me."

To alleviate his loneliness after Hazel died, and because he wanted company, he invited George Bendall, who was then a young minister on the staff at Church Headquarters, to come and live with him in the large house on Lorraine Street. Other than Lena, the cook and housekeeper who had been with Ernest and Hazel for years, and Webb, the chauffeur and handyman, "it was Ernest and me," said Bendall, "in a 26-room house." It was Bendall's job to be available. "I drove him around to the places he wanted to go, and in the evening we would take apart the text and his talks." Bendall said it was a tremendous experience to have had such close personal access to Holmes.

Holmes had expectations of Bendall. "Breakfast is at 8:30 and dinner at 6:00," Holmes told him, "if you're not here you don't eat. I'm not having you move in here to ally-cat around. I want company." On those evenings when Bendall was unavailable one of two other male friends, Bill Knight or Walter Reeves, would come over and sit with him. "He liked having company. He did not want to be left alone."

During the last year of Holmes' life, Bendall saw him as a man in retreat. He wanted to see Founder's church completed, wanted to hear the organ played that was dedicated to Hazel, and wanted to straighten out a few things in the movement. For the most part, however, Bendall observed, "he had lost interest." Holmes told Bendall, "What I've done, I've done. Well, I'm not going to worry about it."

During the last two years of his life, Holmes began seeing more of his brother Fenwicke. Elaine St. Johns says that Ernest and Fenwicke were never really close. "They were never bosom buddies, but after Hazel's death he needed family." Fenwicke used to tire him, Bendall observed. "He still played the role of older brother." When Fenwicke would come to the house in the evening, Holmes would give Bendall money and say, "Go out to dinner. Let's not two of us be bored."

Elaine St. Johns, who knew Fenwicke as well as she knew Ernest, observed that the two brothers were very different, "as different as chalk and cheese. Ernest was earthy, Fenwicke was more esthetic. Fenwicke was definitely a poet, while Ernest was a philosopher. . . . In appearance they were unalike. Fenwicke was small, handsome, deceptively fragile, with a shock of hair that persisted in looking like a halo. Ernest was solid, almost husky, with a determined chin. Fenwicke was (and remained) an academician, proud of his Phi Beta Kappa. . . . Ernest was without formal education and proud of that, a truth-seeker, a debunker, a maverick. Fenwicke was a charmer, an enchanter. When he got into the pulpit he wanted to preach, comfort and inspire. . . . Ernest was a force, sometimes awesome. When he took the platform he wanted to teach you to help yourself."

The differences in the two brothers was also apparent to Bill Lynn, particularly their differing interests. Fenwicke "was always dabbling into something," observed Lynn. "He was into every fad, into diet, vegetarianism and exercise," all of which didn't interest Ernest. In addition, "Fenwicke was never really interested in metaphysical teaching, which was Ernest's passion."

Elaine St. Johns remembers that in the last years Ernest welcomed Fenwicke's visits. While he may have been bored with Fenwicke's dinner-time conversation, "he looked forward to those junkets they made alone in the desert—just remembering." Ernest was a family man, St. Johns recalls, "and he and Fenwicke were all that was left of a large family."

It was at this time that the two brothers worked together on their co-authored epic poem, *The Voice Celestial*. It appeared on the surface to be a shared work. Such was not the case. "It was Fenwicke's idea," says Elaine St. Johns. "Ernest was never bursting to write it. Fenwicke was the moving spirit. Ernest went along with it. If it hadn't been for Fenwicke the book never would have been written." George Bendall watched them work on it when Fenwicke came by the house. "It was all Fenwicke," Bendall concluded. "Fenwicke took out much of the stuff that Ernest had done."[2]

In early 1960 just before he died, Homes came to the conclusion that after his death someone would write his biography. In an effort to provide a base of information, to forestall the perpetuation of myths, and to guard against being "deified or vilified", Holmes engaged Elaine St. Johns to work with him and to conduct a series of audiotape interviews. He died before the project was completed.

After his death the Board of Trustees of the Church of Religious Science decided to carry the project forward and employed Fenwicke to prepare a biography. Elaine St. Johns was hired to guide the project and provide editorial assistance. St. Johns considers Fenwicke to have been the "logical choice" for the job since he was a good writer, knew the early years better than anyone else and wanted to write the book.

The biography, which came to be entitled, *Ernest Holmes: His Life and Times,* took several years to complete and was not published until 1970. It is currently out of print. According to Bill Lynn the project took a long time to complete because it was difficult keeping Fenwicke on track. Fenwicke, according to Lynn, had an expanded idea about the coverage of the book. He outlined a "tome that was far too ambitious, a history of the New Thought movement and the Church of Religious Science." Fenwicke also had the habit, according to Lynn, of upstaging his brother and "taking the credit." That tendency carried over into the writing of the book. Fenwicke had to be reminded "that he was writing a biography of Ernest rather than an autobiography of himself."

Elaine St. Johns disagrees with Lynn's observations, never saw Fenwicke as having a large ego, and denies that Fenwicke wanted to feature himself in the book instead of his brother. St. Johns contends that Fenwicke "wrote with the fulsome and leisurely manner of the 'old school' and quite naturally tended to spend more time on the pre-1924 days of their 'joint glory' rather than on his brother's work in developing the Religious Science movement." She herself found it necessary to cut extraneous material from the manuscript, but it was not because of self-aggrandizement on the part of Fenwicke."

Both St. Johns and George Bendall report that the final chapters of Fenwicke's draft, which dealt with the Institute and the split in the movement, were deleted from the final version of the biography by church officials prior to publication. These chapters "recited things that were going on in the 1950s," recalls Bendall, "and the Board of Trustees did not want them included in the book."

Bendall was still living at Holmes' residence when in early 1960 Holmes became ill. After the Whittier speech in February, 1960, he went to the hospital for tests and it was then learned that he had suffered a liver deterioration and a heart condition. He told Lynn, who had noted a general decline in his health in previous months, that he was not going back to the Institute until he was well. He never returned. Bendall remembers that after he became ill he was often tired. "I had to wake him up in the night and give him his medicine.," he recalled.

Holmes was recuperating at home when, in mid-March, 1960 he had a massive stroke. "I was at the house within an hour after the stroke happened," Lynn recalls. Omar Fareed, his doctor, was called, diagnosed the stroke, and said he would need around-the-clock medical care. "We decided to keep him at home in comfortable surroundings," says Lynn. "Omar probably figured he wouldn't last long." Holmes was never himself after the stroke. "Never to my knowledge," says Lynn, "did he have total coherence, and I spent hours with him."

Lynn was with him the evening of April 7, 1960, when he died, and describes the circumstances surrounding his death. It was early evening when the day nurse had come down and the night nurse had just gone on duty. Shortly after she went into the room she called, "Mr. Lynn, come quick, Dr. Holmes is in shock." Lynn called Dr. Fareed, but Holmes died before a doctor arrived. The official cause of death was, according to Lynn, coronary occlusion.

Dr. Fareed confirmed that Holmes died as a result of complications from a stroke.

Evidently, Holmes was healthy almost until his final days. Fareed, who was his doctor for the last two decades of his life, asserts that Holmes never really had a health problem until 1960. Fareed says, that more than any patient he ever had, Holmes did not want to continue living after his wife's death. His death occurred, says Fareed, "almost as if he willed it."

Bill Lynn, who was the executor of Holmes estate, reports that Holmes left an estate worth about $200,000. He left such a large estate (for that time), according to Lynn and Elaine St. Johns, because he was an astute businessman. He made money as a lecturer early in life, and invested it wisely. Throughout his professional career he had a practitioner clientele of wealthy businessmen. Royalty income from his books also added to his assets. He did not accumulate wealth as a result of his salary as Dean of the Institute. As mentioned above he was paid $10,000 a year throughout his career there. His salary was the same in 1927 as it was in 1960. Since he had no sons or daughters his estate was left to a niece, a nephew, a few close friends and to the Church of Religious Science.

CHAPTER XIV

He Enabled Me To Have
A Wonderful Life

olmes would have led a less stressful life if he had, like his contemporary the mystical teacher Joel Goldsmith, resisted pressures from friends and associates to organize his work and proceeded independently. Managerial adroitness and know-how were not among his strengths. He neither found a successor for himself as head of the movement, nor set up a system for finding one after his passing. His lack of managerial skill led to the organizational split that continues in the movement to this day.

Despite these limitations he realized that without organizational structure his teachings might not survive him. Holmes deserves credit for giving up his preference for maximum freedom of action in his personal and professional life, and for bringing in others to help him organize his work. It was far better to have created some structure around his work, imperfect as it was, than to have done nothing at all.

The testimony of people who knew him personally, as well as the thousands of people who have joined the Religious Science movement in the three decades since his death, clearly indicates that his spiritual teaching has had an important, positive impact. The following is a sample of some of this testimony.

Norman Vincent Peale: "Ernest was a true student, a real scholar, but he was primarily a thinker. . . . There is no question in my mind that Ernest Holmes's teaching helped me on my way."

Charles W. Braden: "He had a rare way of making old theological concepts meaningful in a new way for a changing age. . . . Each of the great ideas he argues and embroiders in a thousand ways."

Fletcher Harding: "His genius is reflected in the fact that he kept the door open so that mankind would not forget metaphysics. Ernest was a significant catalyst."

Shirley McAlpine: "In the context of New Thought, Ernest is the leader of them all. He was an interpreter, he put together the teachings of others to make them understandable. I think he was more concise and learned than the other teachers."

Raymond Charles Barker: "The idea that came through the mind of Ernest Holmes is the greatest spiritual idea in the world today."

Jack Addington: "When I heard Ernest I found for the first time a minister who did not insult my intelligence. . . . He was bringing into the mind of people a new approach to the old philosophies of the Bible and of Emerson."

Peggy Lee: "Ernest Holmes was the greatest spiritual influence in my experience of anyone I ever met. His teachings reached into every corner of my life."

Robert Stack: "Science of Mind is a working philosophy, one you can really use. . . . I think I've never once had the feeling that I wasn't equipped. . . . that I couldn't handle any situation."

Idella Chadwick: (told directly to Holmes himself): "Ernest, you know you've got what I have been looking for all my life. With a teaching background, I've already learned the science of mathematics, chemistry and physics, and since you call this a science, I can learn it. Of course if you had called it a religion, I would have run like the dickens. But Religious Science I can learn."

Robert Bitzer: "One of the most important ideas that Dr. Holmes added to the thought of the time was the idea of definiteness. Prior to this the movement lacked definiteness. Students and teachers sat around waiting for Spirit to tell them what to do. Science of Mind teaches that we are surrounded by a Universal Mind that is creative by nature."

Vetura Papke: "He had a major positive impact on many people. He was a wonderful human being. He enabled me to have a wonderful life."

Appendix

ERNEST HOLMES: CONSCIOUS EVOLUTIONARY
by Noel McInnis

I am moved to take issue with a quotation of Reginald Armor, a man who was close to Holmes for many years. Armor stated that Holmes "was saying the same thing in the last days of earth that he was saying when I first met him."

If we were to take this statement only at face value, we might conclude that Holmes had failed to grow. Yet what the statement truly accords is the lifelong consistency of Holmes' philosophic expression. It does not, however, reflect the *expansion* of Holmes' vision over the years. Holmes progressed from establishing a philosophy of self-dominion of the individual soul, to envision a self-dominioned human species—a shift of consciousness in overall "race mind", not just in individual minds.

In his final book, *The Voice Celestial,* which he co-authored with his brother Fenwicke, there appears the following passage:

> *The future man shall be so far above*
> *The race that walks the earth today he would*
> *Appear among us as a god; yet he*
> *Will be the common man; nor will there be*
> *Such selfish aims as now divide mankind;*
> *Illusion of false values will dissolve*
> *Into their native nothingness and things*
> *Ephemeral and transient of this earth*
> *Shall pass away, and by the second birth,*
> *The field of consciousness shall so expand*
> *All sons of earth shall reach the Promised Land*

At the time these words were written Ernest Holmes had become a *Conscious Evolutionary,* one who understands that human consciousness represents the awakening of a universal consciousness to its overall evolutionary process. Holmes described in the *Science of Mind* textbook the initial step of this awakening, the dawning of self-operational awareness.

> *The first great discovery man made was that he could think. This was the day when he first said, "I am". This marked his first day of personal attainment. From that day man became an individual and had to make all further progress himself. From that day there was no compulsory evolution; he had to work in conscious union with life. . . . As the result of the discovery that he could think, plan and execute, man has built up a great civilization; he has perceived that Nature works through him rather than to work for him.*

Our first great discovery, in other words, was to become conscious of our own personal evolutionary process and its relationship to the larger evolutionary process that we call *nature*. This initial awakening was followed by what Holmes called "the greatest discovery of all time." The mind with which one discerns that "I am", Holmes asserted, is a single, universal mind shared by all thinkers. There is only *one* mind common to all who think with it— one consciousness, one power, one system of universal intelligence, one set of operating principles for the entire cosmos of human experience, whether fathomed, unfathomed for unfathomable. In the context of this totality, said Holmes, "the basis from which man is evolving is Infinite. Behind him is the Great Unknown but not the great unknowable."

The realization of cosmic one-mindedness is essential to our emergence as conscious evolutionaries, for with it comes the awareness that we are localized expressions of a non-local omniscience— that the consciousness in us is concentric with a Universal Consciousness.

We who live today are on the threshold of the next great discovery, that just as Universal Consciousness initially awoke to an operational understanding of its *localized process* in and as us, so in us is it now awakening to an operational understanding of its *non-local* dimensionality. The omni-cosmic dimension of evolution is becoming operationally aware of itself via an expansion of our own self-operational awareness. As scientist George Wald has observed, "Matter has reached the point of beginning to know itself. . . . (Man is) a star's way of knowing about stars."

A conscious evolutionary, therefore, is one who has first discerned that human beings have become the universe's way to learn about itself, in order to assume conscious rather than automatic self-dominion; and who further know and experience themselves as co-participatory in the universe's self-wake-up call.

Along with such notable early conscious evolutionaries as Teilhard de Chardin and Sri Aurobindo (whose *Divine Life* Holmes read annually in his final years), Ernest Holmes was among the first in our era to recognize and teach about our evolutionary role. It was clear to Homes, for instance, that the Universal Consciousness in which we participate is far from finished with fashioning the human species.

Man as we now know him is incomplete, and those vague feelings and subtle senses of interior awareness which arise within him are gentle but persistent prophecies of still greater achievements.

Holmes' vision, therefore, became that of a *world* of transformed individuals. Holmes envisioned the transformation of our entire species and of the planet on which we live. He envisioned nothing less than the emergence of a *new* species. His faith in such a metamorphosis was once asserted as follows:

The world is undergoing the death throes of an old order and the travail of a new birth, and whether or not it remains suspended in a state of indeterminate coma or passes immediately into the Heaven of Divine Promise, will depend entirely upon how many of its ancient corpses it is willing to loose. It is as certain as that the laws of nature are immutable, that some day this transition will take place, someday the world will be reborn, resurrected into a consciousness of unity, cooperation, love and collective security.

Ernest Holmes' prescription for planetary resurrection was delivered in his last annual (1959) Asilomar *Sermon by the Sea*, a prophetic millennial assertion of the role of Science of Mind in bringing about the world's rebirth. In that sermon he declared:

Science of Mind is the most direct impartation of Divine Wisdom that has ever come to the world, because it incorporates the precepts of Jesus, and Emerson, and Buddha, and all the rest of the wise. . . . We have rediscovered that which the great, the good, and the wise have sung about and thought about—the imprisoned splendor within ourselves and within each other—and have direct contact with it. Whether we call it the Christ in us, or the Buddha, or Atman, or just the Son of God the living Spirit, makes no difference. You and I are witness to the Divine fact and we have discovered an authority beyond our minds, even though our minds utilize it.

Just how was Holmes' vision of conscious evolution to become reality? His answer to this question is boldly stated in one of his *Sermon by the Sea's* most striking passages:

It would be wonderful indeed if a group of persons should arrive on earth who were for something and against nothing. This would be the *summum bonum* of human organization, wouldn't it?

Being "for something and against nothing" describes the spirit in which Holmes walked, talked, taught, wrote and lived among the people of his day. This way of being was, for him, the ultimate embodiment of his philosophy, *the* prescription for our conscious evolution:

Find me one person who is for something and against nothing, who is redeemed enough not to condemn others out of the burden of his soul, and I will find another savior, another Jesus, and an exalted human being.

Find me one person who no longer has any fear of the universe, or of God, or of man, or of anything else, and you will have brought to me someone in whose presence we may sit, and fear shall vanish as clouds before the sunlight.

Find me someone who has given all that he has to love, without morbidity, and I will have found the lover of my soul. . . . Why? Because he will have revealed to me the nature of God and proved to me the possibility of all human souls.

Find me one person who can get his own littleness out of the way and he shall reveal to me the immeasurable magnitude of the Universe in which I life.

Find me one person who knows how to talk to God, really, and I shall walk with him through the woods and everything that seems inanimate will respond—the leaves of the trees will clap their hands, the grass will grow soft under him.

Find me one person who communes with cause and effect, and in the evening, the evening star will sing to him and the darkness will turn to light. Though him, as the woman who touched the hem of the garment of Christ was healed, shall I be healed of all loneliness forever.

Find me someone who is no longer sad, whose memory has been redeemed from morbidity, and I shall hear laughter.

Find me someone whose song is really celestial, because it is the outburst of the cosmic urge to sing, and I shall hear the music of the spheres.

Find me one person who has so completely divorced from himself all arrogance, and you will have discovered for me an open pathway to the kingdom of God here and now.

Find me somebody who has detached his emotional and psychological ego from the real self, without having to deny the place it plays in the scheme of things and without slaying any part of himself because the transcendence is there also, and I will have discovered the Ineffable in this individual and a direct pathway for the communion of my own soul.

Where and when did Ernest Holmes expect such people to appear? Who would they be? Holmes' answer to these questions echoes Jesus' admonishment to look neither "lo here" or "lo there":

I am talking about you and myself. When I say "find a person" I don't mean to go over to Rome, or London, or back to your own church. The search is not external. . . . [These] people all exists in us. They are different attributes, qualities, of our own soul. They are different visions; not that we have multiple or dual personalities, but that every one of us on that inner side of life is, has been, and shall remain in eternal communion with the Ineffable where he may know that he is no longer with God, but one of God. If it were not for that which echoes eternally down the corridors of our own minds, some voice that ever sings in our own souls, some urge that continuously presses us forward, there would be no advance in our science or religion or in the humanities or anything else.

Accordingly, Holmes announced his legacy to those who would continue the work that he began:

You are Religious Science. I am not. I am only the one who put something together. I do not even take myself seriously, but I take what I am doing seriously. You are Religious Science—our ministers, or teachers, our practitioners, our laymen. You find me one thousand people in the world who know what Religious Science is and use it, and live it as it is, and I'll myself live to see a new world, a new heaven and a new earth here.

What I am saying is this: There is a Law that backs up the vision, and the Law is immutable. "Heaven and earth shall pass away: but my words shall not pass away." There is a Power transcendent beyond our needs, our little wants. demonstrating a dime is good if one needs it, or healing oneself of a pain is certainly good if one has it, but beyond that, at the real feast at the tabernacle of the Almighty, in the temple of the living God, in the banquet hall of heaven, there is something beyond anything that you and I have touched.

Find one thousand people who know that, and use it, and the world will no longer be famished. How important it is that each one of us in his simple way shall live from God to God, with God, in God, and to each other. That is why we are here, and we are taking back with us, I trust, a vision and an inspiration, something beyond a hope and a longing, that the living Spirit shall through use walk anew into Its own creation and a new glory come with a new dawn.

Ernest Holmes consistently addressed our mind's yearning to know what is so. There are two routes to such wisdom: Those who know themselves comprehend the Universe. Those who know the Universe comprehend themselves.

Holmes' philosophy incorporates both routes, awakening the local, individual self via comprehension of the Universal Self. Science of Mind addresses both those who experience themselves *in* cosmic context, the individual within the universal; and those who experience themselves *as* cosmic context, the universal as individual—the knowing expressed in Holmes statement that "God as us, in us, is us."

It is essential that we, like Holmes, embrace both routes to wisdom. The routes are complementary, not mutually exclusive, and the traveler of a single route is in danger of courting self-diminishment on the one or arrogance on the other. As *fully conscious* localizations of the universal, we become appropriately humble, which means capable of being taught, or as Holmes would say, ever "open at the top" for new learning.

Only as we remain thus open to growth do we avoid diminishment. And thus are we additionally insured against our tendency, when aware of ourselves as the universal in expression, to forget that it is God's part to play us, and not for us to play the part of God. Only as we embody the humility that graces both routes to wisdom may we become fully accountable as conscious evolutionaries.

The occasion for such accounting is at hand, for "conscious evolution" is becoming the meta-curriculum of our time. If Ernest Holmes' philosophy is to be accorded its due place in that curriculum, we are at the fullness of time for the re-visioning of the Science of Mind as Holmes himself re-visioned it.

Notes

1. It Was Not A Planned Thing

1. The term "New Thought" has been applied to the Metaphysical movement which began with P.P. Quimby in the mid - nineteenth century. Adherents of New Thought philosophy see God as an in-dwelling presence, in whom we live, move and have our being. At the core of this belief system is the notion that a new thought embodied in consciousness produces a new condition. Holmes said that the underlying idea running through the New Thought movement was that it was possible to consciously and practically apply "spiritual thought force to the solution of human problems."

2. Webster defines Metaphysics as that branch of philosophy that includes ontology (concerned with the nature and relations of being) and cosmology (dealing with the universe as an orderly system). Webster defines "metaphysical" as relating to the transcendent or super sensible. Fenwicke Holmes correctly observed that the New Thought movement gave the word metaphysics new and special meaning. Ernest Holmes considered it to be the science of mental healing. "The student of metaphysics", according to Holmes, "is learning to consciously control the stream of thought that he allows to enter his inner and creative mentality." Metaphysics, in this view, is a science, and operates under laws of the universe similar to those that govern the physical sciences. "Metaphysics begins," said Holmes, "where physics leaves off . . . . The laws of Mind or Spirit are not different from the laws of chemistry or physics . . . . Metaphysical work rests on the theory that the Universe is a thing of Absolute Intelligence." When the words "metaphysics" or "metaphysical" are used in this book, they are used as Holmes and the New Thought philosophers defined them, not according to the Webster definition of the terms.

2. As A Man Thinketh In His Heart So Is He

1. The quotes from Holmes in the chapter were taken from the books and articles cited in the Bibliography. Many of them were taken from articles he wrote in *Science of Mind* magazine from 1932 to 1955. Especially valuable, as sources of Holmes' thought, in addition to the revised text, *Science of Mind* published in 1938, are the collected essays taken from the *Home Study Course in Science of Mind* edited by Arthur Vergara, and the *Selected Writings of Ernest Holmes* compiled and edited by John S. Niendorff and Kathy Juline.

2. Holmes often used the terms "Science of Mind" and "Religious Science" inter-changeably. He never clearly differentiated their meaning, and made several statements which lead the reader to believe that the terms were synonymous. He once said, "In the study of Religious Science, and *its effective partner* the Science of Mind (italics mine), you are seeking to solve some of the enigmas of human existence." On another occasion he called Science of Mind, "the tool of the Religious Scientist." In the following statement, the term "Science of Mind" could be substituted for "Religious Science" without changing the meaning. "Religious Science," Holmes said, "is a compilation of the great thoughts of the ages, the deep mystical yearnings of minds in search for God, and the modern approach to a faith which can be demonstrated . . . . Taking the best from all sources, Religious Science has access to the highest enlightenment of the ages. Shorn of dogmatism, freed from superstition, and always ready for greater illumination, Religious Science offers the student of life the best that the world has discovered."

3. Mind and Consciousness were synonymous words for Holmes. He once asked, " What is the Mind?" In answering his own question he said, "No living man knows. We know a great deal about the mind, but no one knows what it is. By mind we mean consciousness."

4. Noel McInnis, a minister in the United Church of Religious Science, reports he was told in ministerial school that Holmes at

one time expressed his regret for failing to place greater emphasis on the importance of love in his philosophy of Science of Mind.

5.. Spiritual Mind Treatment as it is now taught in Religious Science churches contains five steps—recognition, unification, realization, thanksgiving and release.

3. I Didn't Make It Up

1. Holmes wrote several articles for *Science of Mind* magazine on the teachings of Jesus. Almost every Christmas season he gave a sermon on the life of Jesus. Most of the quotes from Holmes are taken from those articles which are cited in the bibliography.

2. Holmes addressed the topic of modern psychology in several articles written for *Science of Mind* magazine. They are cited in the bibliography.

3. The quotes from Holmes on PSI phenomena are taken primarily from the first edition of the text, *Science of Mind* published in 1928, and from several articles on psi phenomena published in *Science of Mind* magazine.

4. Craig Carter takes issue with this point. He states, "We were taught not to treat without the consent of the patient, except in the case of children or the mentally incompetent."

4. He Conveyed Something More Than Could Be Said In Words

1. The quotes from Elaine St. Johns, Fletcher Harding, Vetura Papke, William Lynn, Frank Richelieu, Jack Addington, Carleton Whitehead and Craig Carter were obtained from interviews with the author. The quotes from David Bushnell and William H. D. Hornaday were taken from articles which appeared in *Science of Mind* magazine, and the quotes from Reginald Armor from his unpublished manuscript, *Heaven Has No Favorites: The Life of Ernest Holmes as I Knew Him.* (The author wishes to express his appreciation to Armor's daughter, Rev. Marilyn Armor Leo, and to his widow, Elsie Armor, for making this valuable manuscript available.)

2. This biography has benefited from the availability for interviews of several former ministers, staff members of the Insti-

tute and friends who knew Ernest and Hazel Holmes personally during their lifetime. They have shared in great depth and detail their recollections of the life of Holmes and the significant events in the development of the Religious Science Movement. Brief descriptions of how they knew Holmes and became involved in the Movement are provided below:

Jack Addington

A Pasadena lawyer who, after hearing Holmes speak in the early 1940's, studied Religious Science at the Institute in Los Angeles, becoming first a practitioner and then a minister in San Diego. Personally close to Holmes, Addington was involved in the work of the International Association of Religious Science Churches and was an active participant in the church meeting that led to a split in the movement in 1954.

George Bendall

As a young minister in an independent church in New York, Bendall, upon learning about Religious Science, went to Los Angeles in 1953 to meet Holmes. Returning to New York, he brought his church into the Movement. He later joined the staff of the Institute in Los Angeles, and was invited by Holmes in 1959, two years after Hazel died, to live in his home on Lorraine Street. Bendall got to know Holmes both personally and professionally, and had many conversations with him during the last year of his life.

Kendle Bryson

Became involved in the Movement in the 1950s, taking classes from Holmes at the Institute. Became a minister and took a church in Pomona, California, and then in Marin County, California. Knew Holmes only at a distance.

Craig Carter

A former U. S. Marine officer and State Department official who came into the Movement in the 1950s. Became a minister and led churches in Santa Ana and Pasadena. Got to know Holmes personally. Participated in the church meeting that led to a split in the movement in 1954.

Omar Fareed, M. D.

Was Holmes' medical doctor from the mid-1940s until his death. He was raised as a Religious Scientist, his parents having joined the Movement in the 1920s. Socialized with the Holmes' in the latter years of their lives.

Frieda Grinton

She and her husband Lornie, who later became a minister, began attending classes at the Institute in 1946. She became a practitioner in 1951. Spent considerable time at the Institute, getting to know the staff and most of the Los Angeles ministers. Not personally close to Holmes, but conversed with him occasionally, and was knowledgeable about some details of his life

Fletcher Harding

Was a minister of Divine Science in Minneapolis when he met Holmes who was on a trip to Minnesota. Came to Los Angeles and took the church in Riverside after being offered it by Holmes. Joined the Institute staff where he became Dean of the College of Ministers and the first President of the International Association of Religious Science Churches (IARSC). Until he left the Movement in 1953, he was personally close to Holmes, often spending time in the Holmes household.

William Hart

As a ministerial student in the 1950s, and then as a Religious Science minister, Hart knew Holmes professionally. He had an opportunity to observe him at close range in Religious Science classes and at meetings of the Institute staff.

Marian Hefferlin

Came into the Movement in the late 1930s and became a practitioner. Married John Hefferlin, a young minister she met while they were both studying at the Institute. Served as business manager of her husband's church in Long Beach. An admirer of both Ernest and Hazel Holmes, but not personally close.

William Lynn

Was a college student in Los Angeles when he was introduced to the Holmes by his uncle, who was a good friend of both Ernest and Hazel. Taking a liking to the young man, the Holmeses invited Lynn to stay at their home on week-ends and to accompany them on a vacation to Canada. Lived at the Holmes residence during the year after finishing college and getting married. Treated like a son, particularly by Hazel. "I was the little red-haired boy she never had," said Lynn. Joined the staff of the Institute after getting his college degree. Treated like family, he saw a lot of Holmes, particularly after Hazel's death.

Shirley McAlpine

Went to the Institute to study Science of Mind as a teenager in the 1930s. Taking a liking to this inquisitive young woman, Holmes often invited her into his office for talks about his teachings. Became a practitioner, and later, after Holmes death, a minister. Though not personally close to Holmes as an adult, she kept in touch with what was going on at the Institute during the years that Holmes was the Dean.

Oren Moen

Became involved in the Movement in the mid-1950s. Became a minister and joined the staff of the Institute during the last years of Holmes' life. Observed Holmes at a distance, during the time he was spending less and less time at the office.

Vetura Papke

Became involved in the Movement in the 1940s, becoming a practitioner and later a minister. Was on the staff of the Institute in the 1950s and was in charge of the practitioners there. Also served as President of the Practitioners League. Got to know Holmes well, spending time talking with him personally in the mid-1950s and after the death of Hazel. Worked as Holmes' personal practitioner.

Frank Richelieu
Heard Holmes speak in the 1950s and then took classes and joined the Movement, becoming a minister in the late 1950s. A distant observer rather than close personally.

Elaine St. Johns
Personally close to both Ernest and Hazel for over thirty years. Daughter of Adela Rogers St. Johns, one of Hazel's best friends, she was, from the time she was a teenager, in the Holmes social circle. A professional writer, she was employed by the Institute in the late 1950s to help Holmes prepare material which might be later used in a biography. The project was well underway when Holmes died. She then worked with Fenwicke Holmes, who was employed by the Institute to write his brother's biography. She is extremely knowledgeable about the early years of the Movement as well as about the lives of both Ernest and Hazel.

Carleton Whitehead
As a Divine Science minister in Denver, he came to Los Angeles to meet Holmes and decided to join the Movement. Given a church in Monterey in 1952 he became personally acquainted with Holmes at seminars for ministers, and maintained a friendship throughout Holmes' lifetime.

3. Noel McInnis believes this statement needs qualification. See his appendix page 140.

5. *The Formative Years*
1. Most of the material on Holmes' early life was taken from the biography of Holmes written by Fenwicke, entitled *Ernest Holmes: His Life and Times.* A few of the direct quotes from Holmes in this chapter were taken from the "Collected Essays" edited by Arthur Vergara.

6. Working With Fenwicke

1. As in the previous chapter, which deals with Holmes' early life, most of the information is taken from the biography by Fenwicke Holmes. Reginald Armor, who came into Holmes' life shortly after Holmes arrived in Venice in 1912, provided, in his unpublished manuscript on the life of Ernest Holmes, information about the circumstances of Holmes' life during this period.

2. According to Elaine St. Johns, Fenwicke "became a 'star' of considerable magnitude on the East coast. He was one of, if not the most successful New Thought speakers in New York City. For a time he had the Church of the Healing Christ in the huge ballroom at the Waldorf-Astoria, sandwiched in between the founder, Dr. W. John Murray, and the late Dr. Emmet Fox. He had an enormous following. He had many admirers and close friends, among them my mother and myself throughout his life.

7. We Are A Teaching And Healing Order

1. Reginald Armor's two works on Holmes, one of which unfortunately is still in manuscript form, provides important information about Holmes' life after his return to California in 1925, particularly concerning his work in forming the Institute of Religious Science and School of Philosophy in 1927.

2. The minutes of the meetings of the Board of Trustees of the Institute of Religious Science and School of Philosophy (1928-1960) are also a valuable source of information of Holmes' involvement in the growth and development of the Religious Science Movement, as well as on the Institute's finances. Bill Lynn provides valuable testimony about the circumstances surrounding the Institute's financial gains in the 1950s. Robert Bitzer's *Collected Essays* provide information on the establishment of churches.

3. In this quote Robert Bitzer refers to Ernest Holmes as "Dr. Holmes." Holmes had little formal education and did not obtain an academic doctorate from an accredited university. In 1946 Holmes was awarded an honorary degree of Doctor of Philosophy by

India's Andhra Research University for his contribution to religious thought.

8. I've Got A Big Pot Of Stew Just Waiting

1. This chapter was prepared largely from interviews of people who knew Holmes personally. See descriptions (Chapter 4, footnote number 2) for background on how each of the commentators knew Holmes. Reginald Armor's unpublished manuscript on the life of Ernest Holmes was particularly valuable.

9 . He Was Not A Detail Man

1. As in the preceding chapter, the material presented here is largely from interviews with friends and associates of Holmes.

10. We Called Her 'The Duchess'

1. The contribution of Hazel Holmes to the Religious Science movement was evident to several observers, including Elaine St. Johns, William Lynn, William Hornaday, Fletcher Harding, Reginald Armor, Jack Addington and Frieda Grinton.

11. There Is Something Wrong With Our Set-up

1. The Number of Religious Science Congregations by Year from 1939 to 1953:

Year	Number
1939	7
1941	16
1942	17
1944	21
1946	32
1947	35
1948	35
1949	41
1950	46
1951	47
1953	63

2. Report of the Sixth Annual Conference, Religious Science Chapter Association, January 26-30, 1948. Institute Headquarters, 3251 West 6th St., Los Angeles, CA, Robert Bitzer, Presiding.

3. Constitution of the International Association of Religious Science Churches, as adopted January 5, 1949.

4. Letter from S. Arion Lewis to Dr. Ernest Holmes, Los Angeles, April 28, 1948.

5. Report of the Sixth Annual Conference, Op. cit.,

6. Fletcher Harding believes that Holmes felt threatened by these strong leaders and feared that he would be shunted aside if he turned control over to any one of them.

7. Report of the Sixth Annual Conference, Op. cit.,

8. Fletcher Harding, "The New Idea." *Science of Mind* Vol. 22 no 5 (May 1949): 7

9. Letter from members of the Representative Council of the IARSC (signed by Raymond C. Barker, Robert H. Bitzer, Cora B. Mayo, Earl D. Barnum, Jesse V. Longe) to the members of the IARSC, with the salutation, "Dear Friend", February 5, 1954.

10. Annual Congress of the International Association of Religious Science Churches, January 4-8, 1954. This meeting is often referred to as "The Split Meeting." There is a twenty-nine page transcript of a session, held Friday, January 8, 1954, (now in the Archives of the Church of Religious Science, Los Angeles) which provides a record of the discussions between church leaders, including a statement by Holmes explaining his reasons for proposing *The Plan.*

11. Ibid.,

12. Ibid.,

13. Ibid.,

14. Ibid.,

15. Ibid.,

16. Ibid.,

17. Ibis.,

18. Addington himself, speaking with the author in 1991, some 37 years after the event, remembers the confrontation with Arion Lewis,

as being the critical moment, the point at which the split in the Movement took place. While his memory of the course of events is somewhat at variance with the information in the transcript of the Split Meeting, his recollections of what took place are an important source of information about an important event in the history of the Religious Science Movement.

Addington begins by describing events that took place in the fall of 1953, a few months before the Split Meeting. Ernest Holmes called Addington and asked him to get in touch with Jack Fostinis, a member of the Board of Trustees of the Institute, because, as Holmes said, Fostinis "has something to tell you that I want you to know." After contacting Fostinis, Addington was told, "This is not ready (referring to *The Plan*). I can't give you anything on this now. Later on I'll get in touch with you." Addington had not heard from Fostinis when Ernest called again, asking if Fostinis had contacted him. Addington told Holmes, "No. He had not been told anything."

Addington had still heard nothing from Fostinis when just two days before the Split Meeting was to begin, William H. D. Hornaday called and asked if Fostinis had been in touch. When Addington told Hornaday that he was still uninformed, Hornaday invited Addington to have dinner with him on the evening before the 1954 Congress of the IARSC was to begin. It was at this meeting that Addington first learned about the Institute's plan for unification of the Movement. Hornaday then told Addington that Holmes wanted him to make a presentation supporting *The Plan* before the business meeting of the Congress on the following Tuesday.

Addington, after confessing that he still didn't understand exactly what was taking place, was told by Hornaday, that Jack Fostinis would go before the Congress and "explain what we have in mind," and that Addington was to pick it up from there. Addington told Hornaday, "Listen, that's kind of crazy. I don't know anything about this." Hornaday reassured him. "You'll see, it will all work out fine. You just tell how it will apply to your church."

Addington reluctantly agreed, though he suspected it would not be easy. He knew that it would be difficult to understand Jack

Fostinis, who spoke with such a thick Greek accent that "you often could not tell what he was talking about." When the time came for Fostinis to present *The Plan* to the Congress, he went onto the podium, and speaking as fast as he could, according to Addington, "went through all fifty pages . . . . No one understood him."

After Fostinis finished he turned to Addington and said, "Jack, come up here and tell us what this is all about." Addington saying to himself 'this is crazy', got up before the group and said, "Well, I don't know what this is all about. I listened to Fostinis and you listened, but frankly, I didn't get the drift of the whole thing."

Seeing Ernest sitting at the back of the auditorium, Addington, who was still on the podium, asked Holmes if it was possible to have further meetings on *The Plan* and possibly revise it at a later date, so that it would be something all could agree upon. Holmes then turned to Reginald Armor and said, "How about it Reggie. Could we do that?" Armor replied that he didn't know. "Talk to the attorney," said Armor. Addington then spotted Arion Lewis, the Institute's lawyer, in the back of the room and said, "How about it Arion, is that possible?"

Lewis, who Addington remembers had a "bum leg", walked all the way down the aisle, throwing his leg out to the side as he walked, worked his way up onto the stage and over to the podium, and speaking into the microphone said one word - "No."

"This was the moment," Addington recalls, "that the split occurred." The uncompromising attitude of members of the Institute Board alienated many of the ministers and, according to Addington, brought the matter to a head and was responsible for the rejection of *The Plan* by many leaders of the movement.

19 An observation of Fletcher Harding as told to the author during an interview, February 9, 1991.

20. Annual Congress of the IARSC, January 4-8, 1954, Op. cit.,

21. Letter from IARSC Representative Council to membership of IARSC containing "Minority Report" February 19, 1954.

22. Ibid.,

23. Report of Representative Council of the IARSC entitled,

"Analysis . . . Summary . . . Conclusions, on the "New Plan" and the By-laws for same, presented by the Institute at Congress." Submitted to the membership of the IARSC under covering letter dated February 5, 1954.

24. Ibid.,

25. Letter from the Representative Council of the IARSC to the Board of Trustees, Institute of Religious Science, February 16, 1954.

26. The observation of Craig Carter. Of the sixty-three churches of Religious Science, listed in the Directory of Religious Science Churches published in the December, 1953 issue of Science *of Mind* magazine, a total of twenty-six were not listed the following year, indicating that they remained with the IARSC or sought affiliation with neither organization. Thirty-seven of the sixty- three churches joined the Church of Religious Science. With the addition of seven new churches in 1954, the number of Religious Science churches, listed in the December, 1954 issue of *Science of Mind* magazine totaled forty-four.

12. *His Dream Was Not Coming True*

1. The material presented in this chapter has been taken primarily from interviews of ministers and church officials associated with Holmes.

13. *I Want To Get With My Beloved*

1. The material presented in this chapter has been taken primarily from interviews of ministers and church officials associated with Holmes.

2. Bill Lynn disagrees with St. Johns and Bendall on the depth of Holmes involvement. "In his search for inspiration and satisfying activity following Hazel's death," Lynn states, "Ernest dabbled in a number of media—prose, poetry and blank verse. . . It was during this time that he started the writings that became *The Voice Celestial*. He had written some verse previously, but little of consequence. But now he seemed inspired. . . even obsessed! Every morning he arrived at the office with new lines to share with all available. These early writings covered a variety of subjects and

were in a variety of poetic and prose forms. Though perhaps technically not perfect, they were beautiful and possessed a mystical quality, and Ernest seemed perfectly at peace as he read, and recited them to me. Since my office was next to his, and my door always open I got the lion's share of his literary previews during this period. (Others included Willis Kinnear, Bill Hornaday, Edythe Clark, and Reg Armor). His new found enthusiasm delighted us all, and we offered every encouragement to continue. We talked about the direction his efforts could lead. . . perhaps to a modern-day *Pilgrim's Progress.* Ernest realized he knew little about the technical aspects of poetic form. He did some research, but readily admitted he needed help in pulling various verses together, and smoothing them out so that there was a poetic flow. Enter Fenwicke! Ernest had great confidence in Fenwicke's abilities as a writer and editor, and had previously engaged him to edit the scripts for some Science of Mind lessons he was to record for audio books. Fenwicke seemed the logical choice to give Ernest the scholarly editorial assistant he needed and Ernest could provide the financial support Fenwicke needed. Fenwicke took the project to heart. Enthusiastically too! There is no question in my mind that his contribution was great, and essential to the ultimate quality and scope of *The Voice Celestial.* Probably without his help, and encouragement, and nudging, the project might not have reached the publication stage. However, it was Ernest's inspiration, it was Ernest's vision, it was Ernest's ideas, poetry and words that Fenwicke helped weave together with a masterful editorial pen in *The Voice Celestial.*"

14. *He Enabled Me To Have A Wonderful Life*
    1. See transcript of the "Split Meeting", Op cit.,

Bibliography

WRITINGS OF ERNEST HOLMES

Books

1919 *Creative Mind.* New York: Robert M. McBride & Company.

1919 *Creative Mind and Success.* New York: Dodd Mead & Company.

1928 *The Science of Mind: A Complete Course of Lessons on the Science of Mind and Spirit.* New York: Robert M. McBride & Company.

1935 *Questions and Answers in the Science of Mind.* New York: Robert O. McBride & Company (co-authored with Alberta Smith)

1938 *Science of Mind.* New York: G. P. Putnam's Sons.

1943 *This Thing Called Life.* New York: G. P. Putnam's Sons

1948 *How to Use the Science of Mind.* G. P. Putnam's Sons.

1948 *This Thing Called You.* New York: Dodd, Mead & Company

1949 *Words That Heal.* New York: Dodd, Mead & Company

1958 *Help For Today: How to Achieve Security By Using the Power Within You.* New York: Dodd, Mead & Company, (co-authored with William H. D. Hornaday).

1958 *Richer Living: A Proven Therapy for Success Through Right Thinking.* New York: Dodd, Mead & Company. (co-authored with Raymond Charles Barker).

1959 *A New Design for Living.* Englewood Cliffs: Prentice-Hall, Inc. (co-authored with Willis Kinnear.

1978 *The Voice Celestial.* Los Angeles: Science of Mind Publications (co-authored with Fenwicke Holmes)

Articles in *Science of Mind* magazine:

1933 *An Open Letter.* vol. 6 no 7 p 61

1934 *Why Jesus Had Such Power:* vol. 7 no 12 p 82

1934 *An Open Letter:* vol. 7 no 7 p 67

1934 *Man's Relationship to the Universe and the Universal Spirit:* vol. 7 no 10 p 4-30

1935 *The Act of Focusing Attention on a Single Object or Group of Objects:* vol. 8 no 2

1935 *Thought and the Creative Medium:* vol. 8 no 4 p 12

1935 *Inspired by Love, Directed by Intelligence:* vol. 8 no 2 p 7

1936 *What Jesus the Christ and the Mystics Taught:* vol. 9 no 4 p 3

1936 *Dear Friend:* vol. 9 no 3 p 62

1936 *An Open Letter:* vol. 9 no 1 p 66

1936 *God is Conscious Presence and Subconscious Law:* vol. 9 no 3 p 3-11.

1938 *Psychology Spiritualized:* vol. 11 No 6

1938 *We are going to live anyway, but how?:* vol. 11 no 2 p 8

1939 *Good Upside Down:* vol. 12 No 8 p 8

1939 *Of the People, By the People.* vol. 12 No 11 P 5

1939 *God is Not a Person:* vol. 12 no 2 p 2

1940 *The Doctor, Psychologist and Metaphysician:* vol. 13 no 4 p 5

1940 *She Couldn't Get Pupils:* vol. 13 No 12 p 87

1942 *Christmas Message* vol. 15 no 12 p 6-8

1942 *The Light of Truth:* vol. 15 no 12 p 7

1944 *Baccalaureate Address:* vol. 17 no 8 p 11

1949 *The Great Mistake:* vol. 14 no 8 p 9

1951 *This Thing Called Life:* vol. 24 no 2 p 9-10

Talks and Sermons by Topic in *Science of Mind* magazine

Immortality.

Vol. 26 no. 3 (April 1953): 10

Vol. 20 no. 3 (March 1937): 2

Vol. 21 no. 3 (March 1948): 3,

Existence of Hell

Vol. 19 no 4 (April 1946): 12-33

Vol. 6, no. 11 (November 1943): 6

Vol. 19 no. 3 (April 1946): 13

Psychology

Vol. 9 no. 7 (July 1936): 65

Vol. 9 no. 12 (December 1936): 4

Vol. 21 no. 8 (August 1948): 3

Vol. 18 no. 12 (December 1945): 7

Psychic Phenomena

Vol. 21 no. 4 (April 1948): 53

Vol. 24 no. 6 (June 1951): 7-8

Vol. 7 no. 7 (July 1934): 63-64

Vol. 9 no. 2 (February 1937): 5

Jesus

Vol. 18 no. 3 (March 1945): 7

Vol. 18 no. 12 (December 1945): 5-7

Vol. 17 no. 7 (July 1944): 8-9

Vol. 20 no. 6 (June 1947): 46

Vol. 22 no. 4 (April 1949): 5

Vol. 23 no. 6 (June 1950): 10

Vol. 25 no. 12 (December 1952): 5-9

Vol. 16 no. 11 (December 1943): 7

Vol. 14 no. 6 (June 1941): 45

Vol. 14 no. 12 (December 1941): 24

Vol. 10 no. 12 (December 1937): 6

Vol. 9 no. 12 (December 1936)

Philosophy of Science of Mind

Vol. 20 no. 5 (May 1947): 36

Vol. 16 no. 3 (March 1943):

Vol. 21 no. 4 (March 1948): 3

Vol. 21 no. 1 (January 1948)

Vol. 28 no. 6 (June 1955): 3

Spiritual Mind Treatment

Vol. 14 no. 2 (February 1941): 7

Vol. 17 no. 5 (May 1944): 10

Vol. 18 no. 3 (May 1945): 10

Vol. 20 no. 10 (October 1947): 33

Vol. 21 no. 9 (September 1948): 5-6

Vol. 21 no. 11 (November 1948): 5-6

Vol. 28 no. 8 (August 1955)

Vol. 9 no. 7 (August 1936): 65

Vol. 21 no. 2 (February 1948): 89

Vol. 22 no. 11 (November 1949): 9

Vol. 21 no. 7 (December 1948): 7

Vol. 27 no. 6 (June 1954): 41

Vol. 29 no. 1 (January 1956): 4-5

Nature of God

Vol. 28 no. 1 (January 1955): 30

Vol. 10 no. 5 (May 1937): 4, 68

Vol. 25 no. 8 August 1952): 7

Negative Thought

Vol. 9 no. 12 December 1936): 65

Vol. 21 no. 1 (January 1948): 54

Vol. 27 no. 3 (March 1954): 13

Existence of Evil

Vol. 16 no. 2 (February 1943): 9

Vol. 18 no. 3 (July 1945): 7

Vol. 25 no. 7 (July 1952)

Christ Consciousness

Vol. 16 no. 2 (December 1943): 7-8

Modern Medicine

Vol. 21 no. 2 (February 1948): 89

Proselytizing

Vol. 23 no. 3 (March 1950): 16

PUBLISHED MATERIALS

Books

Armor, Reginald. *Ernest Holmes, the Man.* Los Angeles: Science of Mind Publications, 1977.

Awbrey, Scott. *Path of Discovery: The Story of Ernest Holmes.* Los Angeles, United Church of Religious Science. 1987.

Bendall, George P. *The Holmes Papers: The Philosophy of Ernest Holmes.* Manhattan Beach: South Bay Church of Religious Science. 1989

Bitzer, Robert H. *Collected Essays of Robert Bitzer.* Marina del Rey: DeVorss & Company. 1990.

Branden, Charles S. *Spirits in Rebellion: The Rise and Development of New Thought.* Dallas: Southern Methodist University Press. 1963.

Ellwood, Robert S. Jr. *Religious and Spiritual Groups in Modern America.* Englewood Cliffs: Prentice-Hall, Inc. 1973.

Holmes, Fenwicke L. *Ernest Holmes: His Life and Times.* New York: Dodd, Mead & Company. 1970.

Articles

Harding, Fletcher. "The New Idea." *Science of Mind.* Vol. 22 no. 5 (May 1949): 7

Juline, Kathleen. "Ernest Holmes: Founder of Science of Mind, An Interview with William H. D. Hornaday, D. D." *Science of Mind.* (January 1987 10-15)

Kinnear, Charles. "Representative Council at Work." *Science of Mind.* Vol. 22 no. 10 (October 1949): 20

Lynn, William M. "Where Were His Books?" *Science of Mind.* (April 1987): 72

Meredith, Cheerio. "Zest for Living: The Story of Mother Holmes." *Science of Mind.* Vol. 20 no. 8 (August 1947): 6

Parker, Ralph. "Meet Ernest Holmes and the Future." *Science of Mind.* Vol. 19 no. 12 (December 1946): 2-6

St. Johns, Elaine. "One Hundred Years? Impossible!" *Science of Mind.* (April 1987): 35-37

St. John's, Elaine. "Pathways to Positive Thinking: Recollections of Norman Vincent Peale." *Science of Mind.* (June 1987)

St. Johns, Elaine. "Recollections of Peggy Lee." *Science of Mind.* (May 1987): 73

Vergara, Arthur. "You Can Have It All: Recollections of Robert Stack." *Science of Mind.* (March 1987): 73-81

Vergara, Arthur. "Focus on the Ultimate: Recollections of David Bushness." *Science of Mind.* (February 1987): 35-40

UNPUBLISHED MATERIALS

Personal Interviews

Addington, Jack, San Diego, CA., 25 February 1991

Carter, Craig, San Diego, CA, 25 February 1991

Harding, Fletcher, Camarillo, CA., 9 February 1991

Hart, William, Miami FL, 3 March 1991

Lynn, William, San Marino, CA., 27 February 1991

McAlpine, Shirley, Pasadena, CA., 12 February 1991

Melton, G. Gordon. Los Angeles, CA., 6 February 1991

Pitts, Phil, Los Angeles, CA., 26 February 1991

St. Johns, Elaine. Arroyo Grande, CA., 9 February 1991

Vergara, Arthur. Los Angeles, CA., 13 February 1991

Telephone Interviews

Bendall, George. Lake Oswego, OR., 8 February 1991

Bryson, Kendle. Sonoma, CA., 27 May 1991

Fareed, Omar J. Los Angeles, CA, 29 March 1991

Grinton, Frieda. Santa Rosa, CA., 29 May 1991

Hart, William. Miami, FL., 3 June 1991

Hefferlin, Marian. Palm Springs, CA., 27 May 1991

Moen, Oren. Oakland, CA., 27 May 1991

Papke, Vetura. Sun City, AZ., 21 February 1991

Richelieu, Frank. Redondo Beach, CA., 29 February 1991

Whitehead, Carleton. Estes Park, CO., 4 February 1991

Duplicated Material

Armor, Reginald C. *Heaven Has No Favorites: The Life of Ernest Holmes As I Knew Him.* Written in the mid-1970s.

Carpenter, Mark and Johnson, Barclay. *A Conversation With Ernest Holmes.*"March 22, 1956. Typescript of about 100 pages. Archives, United Church of Religious Science. Los Angeles, CA.

Manuscript Collections

Archives, United Church of Religious Science. Los Angeles, CA. Records of the International Association of Religious Science Churches (1948-1954).

Archives, United Church of Religious Science, Los Angeles, CA. Minutes of Board of Trustees. Institute of Religious Science and School of Philosophy. 1928-1935. Minutes of the Board of Trustees of the Institute of Religious Science and Philosophy. 1935-1954. Minutes of the Board of Trustees, Church of Religious Science. 1954-1960.

Archives, United Church of Religious Science. Los Angeles, CA. Minutes of Executive Committee of the Board of Trustees, Church of Religious Science. 1954-1960.

Holmes, Ernest S. Personal Correspondence. 1943, 1960. Archives, United Church of Religious Science, Los Angeles, CA. (There are only two letters in the file. The author was unable to locate the correspondence of Holmes or the Institute of Religious Science and Philosophy for the period 1927-1960. William Lynn states, that, to his knowledge, this correspondence was never retained.

Sound Recordings

McDowell, Catherine. Audio tape of interview with Vetura Papke. November 10, 1986. UCRS Oral History Project. Archives, United Church of Religious Science, Los Angeles.

Leo, Richard and Marilyn. Munson, James. Papke, Vetura. "It all began in Ernest." Audio tape of UCRS seminar at Asilomar, CA 1986. A 146

Index

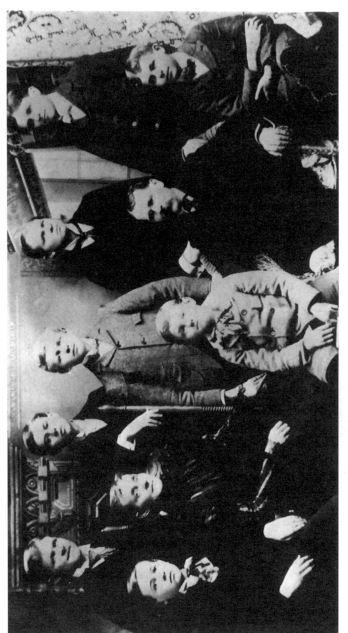

The Holmes family taken when Ernest was about eight years old. First row: Jerome, Anna (mother), Ernest, William (father), and Guy. Second row: Luther, Charles, Fenwicke, William Jr., and Walter.

At age 13.

As a professional
entertainer at age
twenty-five.

With Fenwicke and Mother Holmes in the 1920s.

Fishing was one of his favorite pastimes.

In mid-career.

With Hazel and family dog shortly after their marriage.

With Cecil B. DeMille and Donald Curtis on the set of *The Ten Commandments*.

With Hazel, actress Peggy Lee and the Rev. William H. D. Hornaday.

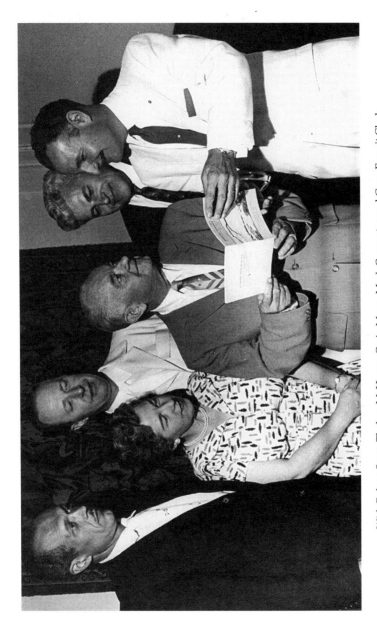

With Robert Scott, Thelma McHenry, Orrin Moen, Mark Carpenter and Gene Emmit Clark.

He loved being with people . . .
(Elsie and Marilyn Armor—wife and daughter of Reginald Armor)

. . . and parties, too!

With Hazel and his mother.

With Hazel and friends.

Comfortable clothes were his preference.

With Hazel about 1955.

With Fenwicke in November 1959, five months before he died.

At the dedication of the Santa Anita Church of Religious Science, January 31, 1960.

Formal photograph, taken during last years.

About the Author

Neal Vahle is an editor and writer living in Mill Valley, California. A Ph.D. in American History, he has written about the lives of people engaged in spritual practice and the development of human potential. While involved for several years with the New Thought movement, he is not a member of the United Church of Religious Science or Religious Science International. He is formerly Director of Heldref Publications, Washington DC and Editor of *New Realities* magazine. Currently, he is on the editorial staff of the Institute of Noetic Sciences, Sausalito, CA.